The Ultimate Direct Marketing, Copywriting, & Advertising Bible

-

More than 850 Direct Response Strategies, Techniques, Tips, and Warnings Every Business Should Apply Now to Skyrocket Sales

The *Largest* and *Mightiest* Collection of Ready-to-Use Marketing Strategies *Ever Published* in the History of the Universe!

Edited by Greg Perry

ISBN: 1523225270
ISBN-13: 978-1523225279

Edited, Compiled, and Improved by Greg Perry

TOPIC CONTENTS

Edited, Compiled, and Improved by Greg Perry

Quick Intro (& Why It's Quick)

This Introduction is short because your time shouldn't be wasted.

To prove we respect your time, please know this: hardly any text you'll ever see that promises to boost your sales fits the standard that *this* giant collection of Direct Response wisdom ever collected in one place gives to you.

That standard is simple:

All stuff and no fluff!

All businesses want more sales. Your only complaint is the sheer number of ways you'll boost your sales *right now* is too much to implement in a single day, week, month, and perhaps year.

But that's okay, do not fret, because if all you did was *skim* this book's strategies for 5 minutes, you'd come away with at least a dozen ways to increase your sales and income *within the next 2 hours*.

Baker or Candlestick Maker

If you're a Copywriter or business owner – you can and perhaps should be both – you'll *immediately* find:

- Short-term Strategies
- Long-term Strategies
- Terrific Tips

- Warnings to Heed

- and Sales-Boosting techniques

that you'll apply to your business right away to make more money in practically every aspect. That business can be a huge retail chain, a local, neighborhood store, a barbershop, an in-home service company, an online empire, or even a family eBay business.

What Business Are You *Really* In?

It matters not what you do because if you don't understand that you are not in any of those businesses actually, but instead, you are in the business of *selling*, then you will never be as successful as you otherwise could be.

Why You Benefit More Here than Any Business Book You've Ever Read

You know the routine. Almost any book or course on copywriting, advertising (advertising is nothing more than selling in print or online), marketing, or direct response that you've ever read never takes you immediately by the hand and tells you straight-to-the-point immediately-helpful items to do right now, in the next three minutes, that will impact your bottom line in a big way. Instead, you've always gotten boring backgrounds, fluff for maximizing page count, and content filler.

The reality is that even the extremely good business books might contain at most a dozen useful strategies.

Not this one. This is the largest collection of immediately-usable selling and business boosting techniques ever released. *Ever.*

No Background, No Filler, No Kidding

Organized by more than 90 topics, from the general (such as Budgets and Money) to specific example businesses (such as Doctors & Dentists, Car Dealers, Plumbers, and even eBay Selling), this this massive collection of selling wisdom was designed to *maximize your income and minimize time you spend implementing each technique out of the hundreds of sales-boosters* given to you right here in these pages.

Here's hoping your income in the next three months tops the previous three years (that's actually a low-level possibility if you implement even 8% of this book's immediately-usable advice)! I sincerely offer you this wisdom in hopes you implement all of it.

Greg Perry, Publisher
MakeRight Publishing, Inc.

P.S. I wish to express my most sincere thanks to Ben Settle, the true master and genius of *All stuff and no fluff,* and the author of scores of marketing titles that have changed the lives and skyrocketed the incomes of countless business owners and copywriters all over the world. I'm continually amazed at the immediate advice I receive daily from his acclaimed Email Players collection (www.EmailPlayers.com).

Edited, Compiled, and Improved by Greg Perry

Ad and Copy

- All advertisements should have 3 parts:

  1. A headline that is a true attention grabber. It reaches out and grabs you by the throat and makes you want to know more.

  2. Ad copy. Can be 25 words to about 600 words that tell you, what it is, where you can get it, what it costs, and what's in it for the buyer. Ever hear "sell the sizzle"? The sizzle is what goes in the ad copy not the features of the product. It is the positioning- who are you comparing your product to. What sells beer? Is it the name of the product? Is it the taste of the product? No! It is the idea that beer = people having fun. That idea is what most people want.

  3. Finally the ad will demand action. Tell your potential customers to do something, buy the product or service, and tell them they must do it now or (fear of loss) it will be gone (this is the ultra-vital time constraint).

- If you have empathy with your customer, you'll be able to write effective ads. This means you must first learn why your customer buys from you (see *Customers*).

- Don't change ads for the heck of it. When an ad works, keep it in place. Test by having other ads, perhaps, but don't replace one that's working well. Test another on a smaller market to see if the first one, the control ad, outpulls the new one or not.

- Never write for a committee. A committee rarely buys anything, individuals do.

- Humorous, abstract, and circuitous ads and commercials are often a waste.

- Fear of loss far outweighs any desire for gain. But try to use both! What your buyer may lose, risk, or waste without your product or service, along with what may be gained or saved if your customer does buy it.

Ad Campaigns

- *After every single sentence* in any ad you ever place anywhere, constantly ad yourself before you place the ad, "Who Cares?" If your ad answers that question, it has potential to make you money. If the answer is only that you do, you're better off flushing your money down a toilet. At least then you won't be surprised that no sales result.

- When critiquing advertising, always begin with "Who Cares?" Then get as nasty as you can. This makes for a *great* and constructive ad critique. Also ask, "Why should I believe you?" and "Why should I do this now?" If you put those self-imposed questions to work, you will be a great copywriter and you will sell things.

- The terms, *no theory, taught from experience, just proved real-world results!* All go together nicely if your copywriter can craft them together in context of your ad. (good for sales letters)

- In ads, it's often good to reveal a flaw. This should be a cosmetic flaw and not structural problem. Such as, "I only have this in Red," or "it has a 350-radio speaker system but does not have voice-controlled tuning." In long ads, *always* do this. Stated flaws make you more believable.

- If you state one or more of your flaws (or your product's or your service's flaws) and how you overcome it makes your potential buyers more confident. They instinctively feel that if you reveal a problem or two, then you're far less likely to be hiding something else from them.

- Businesses get tired of their own ads far sooner than clients. How many times do you look at car ads? You look when you buy a car but not all the time. So a car dealership finds a successful ad and they shouldn't change it until a better one is proved. You can test other ads in other papers, or run an "A-D" ad where half the papers carry the proved ad and the other half carry another to see if the second outperforms. But don't get rid of the performing one just because *you* are tired of it.

- Advertising is salesmanship in print. Never say what a top salesman would never say when speaking directly to a potential buyer.

- An ad campaign consists of various phases. Getting the ad placed is just the beginning. Ads should be tested – no, *must* be tested.

Consider placing new ads in the *free* or low-cost

classifieds section before you purchase space. (True for both offline as well as online (Craigslist before Google Ads, etc.) If the ad pulls there, you have evidence that it should produce results in paid advertising venues.

- There was once a story about a town that had a fund-raiser to bring a rainmaker into the town to make it rain. Before the rainmaker came there, was a big town prayer meeting to ask God to prepare the way for the rainmaker to bring rain. On the day that the rainmaker arrived in town, one small child came to the town-square with an umbrella. This indicated that the town had faith in God, the rainmaker, or both. This indicated that perhaps the most innocent might be able to see through to reality that others cannot.

  So did it rain? Maybe, maybe not. The marketing moral of the story is to know exactly how you are going to handle responses, positive and negative. This could include an auto-response message you set up. It could be putting the right message on your voice mail, or training your staff into handling the calls to filter down to the caller's actual desire.

- Know the demographics of the magazine or Ezine or social media target group in which you place your ad. Does your product appeal to your desired target market? You could have the best ad ever written, but if it's placed in the wrong media, you will get no response.

As an example, suppose you had a product that appeals primarily to women but then placed an ad for it in a man's magazine. This is rather an extreme example, but mistakes like that occur too often. The business blames the ad or blames advertising when it's their lack of understanding marketing principles of targeted ads that was the sole problem.

- It seems obvious but is constantly ignored: Ad timing is important. A message that has a great response in November may not have the same appeal in June. The reasons people buy can be quite seasonal for many products.

- Always set up buying criteria for your customers. It's like sending out a free report saying, "Do *not* buy XYZ until you determine that the seller follows 5 key principles"; then, ensure that *your company* does all five.

- By setting the buying criteria, you eliminate the following customer's perceived problem: "I don't have any need for your product" and that may be true but the buyer rarely has considered all aspects of that decision. So make the customer want to consider all aspects of going elsewhere or doing nothing.

- When customers call but don't place an order, tell them that's okay… But before they buy from *anyone*, check them out and make *sure* that they hear you help them avoid future buying decisions by offering them buying criteria that your company strictly adheres to.

- When you set up buying criteria as "5 things you *must* understand before you buy ...," say no matter who the buyer ends up buying from, make sure "that they adhere to environmental standard 5C-17 to eliminate as many allergy symptoms in your family as possible." (Obviously, you will structure your criteria to meet your company's products and services.)

  While it may be true that many of your competitors also adhere to those same standards, those competitors won't understand the importance of explaining that to their potential buyers. In telling your potential customer that it's fine that they wait, but to be sure when they *are* ready that they don't mistakenly ignore those criteria factors. You will develop a great deal of trust in doing this, and often you will get the sale then.

  Even if you don't get the sale, that potential customer will always remember that you guided him into making a wise purchase decision when it does come time to purchase.

- It's "old school" but never forget it: Use *AIDA* - *Attention* (such as grabbing your target's attention by using their title "Homeowners" and a headline that zaps them), *Interest* (don't assume you your target knows your product's or service's benefits; explain the benefits, leading with the top benefit), *Desire* (explain the needs that you or your product will fulfill), and *Action* (a definable offer and a call to action step; when a customer is never told to do something, the customer typically does nothing.)

- More words *always* outsell fewer words and a picture. Obviously you must have something to sell, you must know how to craft copy, and you understand that you're selling a need and never a product or service. Don't make something look too slick. A full page ad from a bank with nothing but a dove flying in the center of all white with the words, "We free you," may be artistically stunning (it's not though) but an ad that begins with, "We might lose your money" could actually pull more. Be effectively creative with your copy, never be artistic at the sake of tried and true copy.

- Don't hide problems in your ads. As stated before, explaining problems and how you overcome them builds confidence. The flip side, however, is that if you're not fully honest with a flaw that a new customer is going will see right away after the sale, that customer will be surprised in a negative way and never trust you again.

- Show your warts! Consider James Webb who sold fruit by mail order about the time Harry & David began. A hail storm bruised his apple crop but did not damage them. He was afraid he would have too many returns. So he enclosed a letter with each order saying something like, "Note the pockmarks on each apple! They are proof they have been grown at a high mountain altitude where the same extreme cold that causes sudden hailstorms also firms the flesh and increases the natural sugars. This makes the apples even sweeter." The next year, some customers complained because their apples didn't have the marks!

- If you use magnetic sign ads on your car, it is more important where you *park* than where you *drive* if your ad is internet-centric such as promoting a web site. Parking, say, in front of the windows at an Internet café or library, means anyone with real interest may likely look you up as soon as they get to the WiFi with their laptop or tablet.

- You can also reveal a flaw in yourself as the business owner. Such flaws make you more believable and more personable. (Explain how you overcome the flaw.)

- Just have a conversation with customers in your ads. Use their favorite word, "you," a lot. It's just you speaking to a potential buyer.

- You may not always be able to work out a per-result advertising cost basis, but review all your professional and advertising expenses and attempt to put as many of them as possible on a shared revenue or cost-per-result basis. An ad with no feedback mechanism, such as most billboards, means you will never know how many customers that no-direct response ad did or didn't bring in.

- Learn your audience's secret fears, worries, spousal worries, etc.

- Always be "one of the guys" to another guy.

- You must make test ads targeting starter clients. Some ads bring in fewer clients but generate far more purchases and you must test this and hone it to find the sweet spot.

- If you mess up and make a mistake of some kind, put it in your next headline, saying "We Goofed!" People can't help but read what you did.

- For short print/eZine/web page ads, to get initial response: 1. State the big benefit and don't make it subtle but spell out exactly what you're giving ("*Free* Report shows how to…" "Stop the pain of …" "*New* report stops your…NOW!") because people buy benefits and not features, 2. differentiate the product ("Free Report shows you *Everything*….," "Stop guessing at…"), 3. Give action to perform (a link, phone, or email address).

- *Only* if your ad/sales letter has an action step can you track how effective the device is! Generic institutional advertising has absolutely no way to track advertising results.

- For online ads and sales letters, put an order link or button close to top "above the fold" (differs some from print advertising).

- Ads and letters: never *ever* put more than six sentences in a paragraph and two or three is a better count. Can there ever be an exception? Certainly, but it's an exception that proves the rule.

- The one who teaches his market *how* to buy (such as teaching them data about the product that *they* sell (that they buy from you), and teaching them about their own customer demographics, and so forth) is the one who sells the most. Scare your prospects about your competition! Make them afraid to buy from someone else who won't teach them and who don't make them preeminent. Find out *what* in your market makes you more important to deal with than just your product. Research your customer's needs and market! Provide freebies that help them do business that your competitors won't. If it's disposable (such as a yearly thing, perhaps a trade show calendar in their area but one that has helpful information and not just your logo and pictures), then they will begin to rely on you regularly.

- Never run institutional advertising. Always give an action for your clients to do something.

- Use *because* a lot in your copywriting, followed by a compelling reason to do something. The combination is a powerful way to produce a "reasons why" buyer response.

- Too many people say "Buy from me! Buy from me!" They forget to say... "Because...:" They fail to educate their customers. A "reason why" is worth gold.

- Negotiate when buying advertising or professional services so that you only pay for results (and you'll pay more for results that are great, more than the professional would have charged for routine, general services; that's fine). Perhaps your local TV station has unsold ads late at night, and you can offer to pay only for results brought in directly from that ad space. Perhaps buy magazine advertising only for results brought in.

  All this moves the risk off your shoulders onto those who are selling you something (the advertising supplier). Your best bet to talk them into this successfully is to cover their downside costs at least as well as show a high probability you can bring in orders. The words that print advertising knows (and dislikes) are "per inquiry" and "per order" but you'll get better response from the advertiser if you use the words, "shared revenue." (Means the same thing but they don't feel what they consider to be the sting of "per order" ads.) Perhaps you pay on money saved.

- Replace all non-accountable professionals you pay with people whose fees are strictly performance-based in some way. This takes creativity but boosts your business and your employee's incomes in the long run.

- An ad is a sales pitch in print; it is not fine art, not creativity in the standard way of thinking.

- Generally, radio ads are good for lead generation but not for direct sales. Generally.

- Match to someone's expectation levels. You've seen ads that say, "Make $500, $1,000, $10,000, $100,000 your first month in business!" Those levels allow the reader to inquire up to his actual expectation. If you only put one number, you filter out too many potential buyers.

- A good copywriter, when looking at the results of any ad, only tells you how well it pulled. The esthetics of the ad is not a goal in any way.

- In your copy, tell stories, then add more stories. Give your stories interesting characters and dialogue, plus a dramatic lesson that your prospects can relate to. Don't' say, "Certain companies have used our software." Don't even say, "IBM has used our software." Instead, say "Joe Smith, at IBM, said to me, 'If we don't increase sales turnover by 20%, we won't make our projections.' We guaranteed they could just that if they used our software. Six months later, Joe called and said, 'You guys saved us.'"

- The better newspaper ads appear either on the front page or the back page of a section.

- Don't make newspaper or website ad look like an ad. Make it look like an editorial or news story. Make sure you have a killer headline, but also killer sub-heads throughout and have the ad span top and bottom of fold. Your sub-headings grab the readers who don't look at the top of the fold while separating out their favorite sections.

- On buying ads on Web sites: Do a search of google.com and bing.com for the item you sell (such as "fuel filters") and see how many hits come back. Get more specific. Try to get a feel for whether or not there are a lot of sites to advertise on or only a few. If only a few, then you must have a high-dollar product for it to work. Perhaps you get more general (such as food sites if you sell cookies) for ad places versus targeting only sites that sell cookies.

- Your Ad or sales letter (same thing, an ad is salesmanship in print) should be what Jay Abraham calls a "greasy chute" because once your customers start it, they should be compelled to keep reading as though they are sliding down into a greasy chute that they cannot stop. The letter should pull the customers with it voluntarily.

- In ad, sales letter, or web site, don't specifically say what you will do as in, "I will do this..." and "We will do this..." Make that obvious but implied. Let your writing show the reader you will do those things without making it so explicit.

- Creative marketing belongs to the one who tells the potential customer exactly why the product should be purchased.

- Suppose you sell curtains that you make. In the process, three times a year your company's buyers go to Manhattan or Paris and they sift through thousands of samples looking for ones that suit *your* particular customer desires and needs, and they look through 50,000 products but only select 100 that ends up in your catalog.

Tell your customers this in your ads. Maybe that's what *every* competitor does too, but you'll be the only one who educates your clients properly if you tell them exactly what you've done. You'll get the sell.

- Be very specific on an action plan. Give them a reason to act and act *now*.

Edited, Compiled, and Improved by Greg Perry

Affiliate/Associate Programs

- Have your vendors sell your product, or at least recommend/endorse your products, to their customers. Give them an incentive.

- Let's say you sell well your front end. When you begin selling your back end, go to other business owners and tell them, "Look, I made $XXXXX selling this product to *my* list. Let me sell them to your list and I'll pay you a 65% commission." (You want the back end sales so you'll gladly do this with your front-end product.) *The money is in the list - the money is in the back end.*

Edited, Compiled, and Improved by Greg Perry

Autoresponders

- Autoresponders, such as Aweber.com, are gold for many businesses, yet only a few are aware of their existence and how to use them.

- If you put a different autoresponder code on each web page of your site (the major pages) you learn quickly which pages are most effective and most visited.

Edited, Compiled, and Improved by Greg Perry

Back-End

- The *real* money is usually in your back-end product.

- If you have no back-end product, work on providing add-on products for a while. Once you have several in your inventory, combine them all for a comprehensive back end product.

- Always have a back-end, high-priced item. Sell a front-end, under-$100 product (easily ordered online is the best), then sell your high-cost back end to your customers.

- As a back-end, you can endorse other people's products in your follow-ups with a commission agreed to in advance between you and the other marketer. Be sure you share lists and he does the same for you.

- Especially for high-priced back-end items, mail multiple mailings called *sequential* or *multi-step* mailings.

- All money is in back end, but you can sweeten the front end to make the back-end easier to promote. Let's say you make $200 profit on a $400 item. Find something like $100 of season tickets to the local team, or a famous seminar, or something you can buy in bulk discount, perhaps offering the seller $5k for all unsold tickets and you end up only paying $35 per ticket but it has a higher perceived item. With each front-end sale, you can give away the $100 ticket that only costs you $35. You give up $35 to add $100 perceived value to your item.

- You don't really need an *actual* back-end product as long as you have affiliation to sell back-end products that someone else offers. For example, a car information web site might promote and sell used car warranties, even though the owners of the site have no contact or actual experience in used car warranties. They leverage the experts who do have the experience and insurance products, getting a commission for each referral or sale.

- No back-end product? No? Well, then make what you sell *now* a back-end item, add some value and raise its price, and create another product that gives you a better front-end which brings in more leads.

- If you don't think you have a back-end product, you're fooling yourself. A back-end adds value to the total result for the customer. You don't have to make the product, perhaps another company brings you a product or service you can use as a back-end. You can determine, if you know your customer's worth, how much you'll pay for that referral for a back-end.

- A referral, when sought after, could very well be considered a back-end sale for your business.

Bartering

- Considering barter for lower advertising rates or whatever you need: Your goods and services cost you far less to produce than you sell them for. So, if you can trade a good or service for another good or service, you end up paying wholesale for that item.

- Trade for full retail value (both yours and the company you barter with) and not a discounted price the company might sell for during sales.

- You can barter via *triangulation*. Suppose you want advertising but the advertisement owner doesn't want your good or service. Find out what they do want and barter someone else for that.

- Always insist on assignability for the bartered item or service that you receive a credit for. Remember, too, never try to trade your goods or services at anything less than retail value. Remember, the higher the valuation you place on the goods or services you trade, the greater your buying advantage.

- Develop relationships with competitors on some level. If a client's leaving you anyway without purchasing, if there are several competitors in town and you have a relationship with one of them, get a referral and get permission to cut the deal yourself or tell them you'll pay xx% of whatever they buy from there as long as that xx% is less than your before-the-deal agreed on price reduction with the competitor. Make the same offer to the competitor. You'll both bag sales that could have easily gone to a third party.

Benefits

- Specific claims increase believability. Do not advertise, "This car gets great gas mileage." Do write, "This car gets 41 miles per gallon in the city and 52 mpg on most road trips."

- Don't promise too much on a hard dollar amount (such as, "Puts $500,000 in your pocket within 365 days"). If you are targeting a group of firemen, for example. Be careful not to mention a dollar amount more than about double their annual salary. You can add qualifications of how they might make much more, but the primary benefit needs to be a reasonable number to your target audience. And let's face it, anything much more, and you do lose credibility.

Edited, Compiled, and Improved by Greg Perry

Book

- If you have a book about you, your business, or for your customers (see *Business Cards*), offer a free downloadable item inside the book. This gets people to your web site. (Do this more than once throughout the book.) On the actual landing page, offer an upsell item that compliments the freebie.

Edited, Compiled, and Improved by Greg Perry

Brochures and Catalogs

- Too many people try to cram everything in an ad or brochure or catalog page to "get the most bang for the buck." Unless they are *very* good at catalog design (such as *Lands End*), they'd do far better to limit one or two products to focus on.

Edited, Compiled, and Improved by Greg Perry

Budgets

- During recessionary times, most companies cut back on their most important area – *Marketing*. So if you want to destroy your competitors, you should market heavily when they are not.

Edited, Compiled, and Improved by Greg Perry

Business

- "What business are you in?" if you answer *any*thing other than Marketing, you don't know what business you're in.

- Ask yourself this question about your business: "What would we do differently if we charged admission?"

- Hardly any business knows statistics from its own industry. If you sell shoes, for example, differentiate your product by learning about your industry, know how many men have bought shoes in the past year, how many women, how many women, break it all down by age, by salaries, and so on. Learn that someone who earns $100,000 typically has XX shoes, so if you want to earn $100,000 a year, then you need XX number of shoes in your closet (*ha-ha*, kidding). Industry statistics enable you to help differentiate yourself and to use those statistics to set up buying criteria for your customers who may initially be unwilling buyers.

- Although this is a business-specific tip, it's a perfect example of the out-of-box thinking that all businesses should entertain: Women's dress shops should have a men's room with videos, internet, whatever. That also opens the market (pop machine and coffee at *least*) for selling items such stores would normally never be able to sell)

- Ask yourself these questions:

- Why did you start your business? (i.e., "I got into business because...")

- When you first started out (*waaay* back if needed), how did you attract your first customers? The process and the single application that got your real business. A basic process that got your business to a certain level, then it got bigger and maybe you became a manager, but at a certain level of critical mass you stopped doing something, perhaps a part-time person did it for you, and after that point, you cannot understand why your business stalled. Write it down, the complete thing you did more than anything else, that got you customers. *Be specific* (not just "direct marketing" or whatever).

- Now, look at the other side of the transaction. As specifically as possible, why did your customer buy from *you*, (originally when you began). Learn what you provided, perhaps, that others didn't or couldn't. Dissect what you had done that made them want to do business with you.

- Why do they buy from you *today*? It may the still the same reason as the previous one, but it's likely different. Soul search here.

- Almost all industries use a similar approach to get customers. If you isolate industry A to see what they do to drive their business, you can almost say, "Their primary mode of getting customers is XXX" (Shopping centers might be location, fliers, etc. A doctor may be referrals. For car dealership it's perhaps newspaper, billboards, and TV.) Think of your industry, if it's a reasonably large industry, would we be correct in assuming that 90% or more businesses in your industry do the same thing? If true, and it is, then in *your* business, what is your current primary mode of marketing? You may do many things, but *one* primary approach accounts for the bulk of your time, effort, and results, so what is it? Be very specific.

- What services or product do you offer? What are the advantages and benefits? What is your front-end? What is your backend?

- What do your customers often want that you do not provide? (If your employees are not trained to keep a journal of goods and services asked for but not for sale at your location, you're missing out on valuable, direct, cash flowing income by not knowing some things you should be providing that you never thought about before.

- What would make your product irresistible?

- What is your competition like? Analyze their name, product, abilities, and customer service.

- How does your company compare to the competitor(s) above?

- What financial goal do you have for your company in five years? What are you doing to prepare for this to happen? Do you have the infrastructure to handle this?

- Describe your company as a person: gender, personality, character.

- What are your three primary methods for generating prospective sales? How do you get your leads?

- How many customers/clients do you now have in your database?

- How many "dream" clients are there?

- Out of 10 prospects, how many will you close? This is your closing ratio.

- What do you do with the prospects you don't close? (Sending them to a competitor you've arranged a finder's fee for could be an interesting thing to try; certainly it's better than them going there without you getting a referral fee.)

- How do your closing ratios fare against competitors?

- Describe five of your most typical purchasers. (You'd better do this now if you haven't.)

- What are the top three reasons that you lose business to competition?

- What follow-up do you do with clients after they buy?

- Do you ask for referrals and how?

- If you have salespeople, what are your standards for hiring them? What training do you offer? What would make the sales training excellent? Do you learn why your top salespeople are at the top and if so, do you teach the others what to do?

- How many times do you send your clients info that is *not* about your product? (Informational, personal greetings at holidays, and so on.)

- How do you educate your clients? Do you provide seminars? Newsletters? Sponsor events?

- Where do you advertise?

- How much is a customer worth in the first new sale, the first year, and the lifetime?

- What does it cost you to get a new customer?

- What do your competitors do best? What do they do worst?

- How much of your business comes from referrals?

- Do you ever acquire a customer at break-even up-front so that you can make a profit on the back end?

- What is your referral system?

- How do you guarantee through risk reversal?

- How long is your guarantee for each product?

- What are your yellow page and online ads like?

- How do you up-sell and cross-sell?

- Do you package complementary products and services together?

- Do you increase your prices to see how it works?

- How many other people's products do you endorse to your customer base?

- Do you buy from competitors to keep track of what they're doing right and wrong?

- Do you actively seek experts in your field and fields related to yours? How?

- What is your Unique Selling Proposition? (Why customers buy from you, what distinguishes you from the crowd, and so on.)

- Have you made your USP a consistent theme in all your marketing and sales efforts?

- What is your selling season if you have one? Have you researched other products or services for your slower periods?

- How loyal are your customers? Is that higher, normal. Or lower than your industry?

- Do you ask your customers constantly what they want and need from you? How often do you do surveys?

- How many inactive customers are on your list? How do you activate them once again (free offers, stop-by-for-snacks-parties, and so on).

- Do you constantly ask *why*? Why did someone buy from you, why would I be competitive, why should my customer buy from a competitor over me, why would my customer see me as being better than competition?

- Is your company *very* local, like a 3-mile customer radius? Perhaps make a video with owner being interviewed and distribute them on USB thumb drives or DVDs door-to-door. Include a short note attached nicely saying, "return this *short* 9-minute video having watched it, and bring it to our company and we'll give you a free XXXXXXX just for having watched it and returning it. NO obligation, no pressure to buy, no phony, no baloney."

- If you have a business, such as a car dealership, and you don't have a free report that says, "*Warning*: Seven things you *must watch out for* before buying from a used car dealer," (and you make sure you've come up with seven things only you can fulfill (a possible USP foundation), then you are giving away business to your competitors. Such a free report, however, means you *have no competitors*. You now are not one who puts down your competitors – you now have none because you're the only one who meets such important criteria.

- If you're an Electrician or in any other home-service occupation. Look around when you do any job. If you truly see something more you can do for your customer, especially large, unless you are in a time-crunch, tell the client about if and that you will charge them a special reduced fee because you're already on site. If they balk at the cost, then give them terms and take only a down payment (that should cover your costs). Tell them that you can come back at a later time when they have more money but that you'll have to charge the usual fee, although since they are following your advice you will also toss in something extra. If they still balk at the price but realize it's an important job, tell them that they are important to you and give them the name of a competitor and tell them he won't might not warrant his work as well as you but that he will charge less and that even though it's your competitor, your customer is most important to you. Obviously, if you've worked something out with that type of competitor in advance for a referral, that last alternative is not bad for you. Whatever you do, tell the client you will contact the competitor yourself and explain what needs to be done and that he needs to give you his rock-bottom price (and you can get a referral fee then).

- Want to be the number one business in your field in the nation? Even if you're a one-person business? Here's one possible way to achieve that: Make your customers feel unconditionally loved and not in some phony, contrite way. And do it for your employees also.

- Focus your business. Don't be all to all. The more you focus, the more sales you'll make, the better you'll understand your target market, and the better you'll sell to your target market.

- The strongest worker in a company is the owner. The owner can leverage his or her abilities by cloning yourself, perhaps in a video. You can be interviewed. Hire a television station to interview you for material. This is a great thing to give customers for insight into why you value them and it's extra important for your employees to know more about your goals, views, and why you run the business the way that you do.

Edited, Compiled, and Improved by Greg Perry

Business Cards

- Put an action step on every card. That way, the recipient will not want to put it in their wallets but somewhere they can find it.

- Your card *must* have a call to action. Perhaps it's a free autoresponder report. You *must* put your unique offer or service in 17 words or less on your card

- Don't put your company name in the card's upper-left corner but put what you do (Day Care Center – bold upper-left corner), state your #1 benefit, email address for free report or some action. Your company name is actually the least important data on your cards.

- If the back of your business card is blank, *are you nuts?* That's valuable real estate that you could use for a special offer, a helpful tip for a potential customer, or a link to a problem you solve on a web page. Those are things that bring you business… Why would you ever leave half of your business card blank?

- A book makes the most powerful business card on earth. You need a book that you give away which explains why you succeed, how you help, tips, and lots and lots of links directly back to you and your business. You don't need to know how to write to get a book published, check eLance.com for tons of writers willing to work with you to produce a book for a low amount.

- An actual book written by you is the best business card possible. As said above, eLance.com can ghost write your book if you can't write, just send a list of things you want in there. If you can't type but are good at speaking, dictate a book into a recorder and send the file to eLance.com to get it transcribed and then hire a writer to turn it into an edited, readable, consistent book.

  Note: In the book industry, it's perfectly find to have "your own book" that was actually written by someone else. You don't have to say who the co-author (the actual writer) is, unless that is part of your agreement when you hire him. If so, you only want to say, "With John Brown," not "Co-authored by" on the book itself.

Car Dealers

- On your web site, email, and yellow page ad, always provide a link to a letter that says, "Warning! Don't buy from *any* Used Car Dealer until you read this!" then explain why you are the only one they should do business with.

- Have your yellow page ad typeset by someone other than phone company so you know it's picture perfect and that it doesn't look like everybody else's.

- If you buy a full-page yellow page ad, ask for free smaller ads placed throughout rest of yellow pages; these are often available for large ad buyers.

- Telephone a week after selling a car to sell an extended warranty plan if your customer didn't buy one.

- Car lots would do well with a better trade-in offer when a buyer brings a car that he bought before than from *you*, as opposed to a trade-in bought elsewhere. A return customer is far easier to sell than a new one.

- Target groups of people who need what you have, such as taxi companies, that you'll sell to at a discount, or at a fixed price over Blue Book or whatever.

- If interested customers have a good-selling car or a classic worth an extra- good margin to you if they trade it in, send a letter FedEx to that special customer list with a sales letter for the product, have a private showing to them with cheese, crackers, and one-on-one showing.

- Obviously sending a gift certificate for a car-detailing would be a great follow-up to a car sale. Always make a deal with the detailing company you use to get a discount since you'll be sending all your buyers there. Work it out so that you only pay for certificates redeemed, not for the certificates you send out. And... of course, the detailer should, for their very best clients, have deep discount certificates that you provide for *your* business.

Carpet or House Cleaning

- A carpet cleaning company could offer lifetime cleaning for a furniture store's upholstery. Let the furniture store sell the lifetime cleaning as a free bonus for the furniture. Then, the carpet cleaner gets all kinds of back-end sales from the subsequent cleanings. You go to clean the furniture bought for free, but you'll more than likely get a carpet cleaning job out of it. Once you get a carpet-cleaning job, you know how to follow-up for routine, preventive maintenance carpet cleanings in the future. Give them a carpet-cleaning discount if they let you set up a regular furniture and carpet cleaning.

- Have a drawing and *three* of the winners will get a free, complete, entire-house cleaning. No obligation, no money accepted, completely free just to get their business name out. Those who enter only need to have their carpet cleaned! So you have a re-hot mailing list. Send a letter to those who don't win and offer them a deep discount as thanks for signing up. Then, when you get there, sell them a maintenance contract for a multi-service, less-per-service fee.

- Send a free coupon for *one room free cleaning*, no other obligation. Offer them a discount on other rooms.

- Contact furniture companies for upholstery and carpet cleaning.

- Approach real estate brokers for one-half house carpet cleaned free of anyone selling their home. Anybody who follows up later received a $25 gift certificate or check or donation to charity to the recommending broker.

Classified Ads

- A classified ad is really nothing more than a headline and information on how your potential buyer should follow up. Any other kind of print ad is a "display ad." (Display ads are best done as articles that look exactly like surrounding articles. In newspapers, the best place for one is often at the bottom of the business or sports page (yes, beneath the fold) and make it look exactly like the other articles. If *you* put in tiny, 5-point or some other extremely small font "Advertisement," the newspaper people are less likely to do it themselves (where it will be larger). But even if they do it, this will not hurt you much at all given the huge number of people who will read the article (if the headline is newsy *and* is also a powerful sales letter headline at the same time). Start such display ads with a quote from someone.

- Always use a bold headline in a classified. Pay for one blank line, the bold headline, then one more blank line, then the rest of the ad. Your ad will stand out!

- Even better, buy 2 or 3 times the classified space you need but use only the center of it (putting several blank lines at the top and bottom of your copy). Then, request a hand-drawn circle around your ad. Nothing will catch the classified readers like your ad.

- Free recordings (or audio easily played on Web) make for great offers to get leads.

- The only reason for a classified ad is to generate a lead.

- Non-classified newspaper ads should look like articles, be thin, and run longer than one-half page so it appears above *and* below the fold. Also, sub-heads should be used to catch people's eyes who read the half below the headline. Wrap up the end that basically just restates the headline for those people.

Client & Customer Service

- Always look at your idea, business, product, newsletter, postcard from the customer's viewpoint.

- The founder of Zapos, the shoe site, once called his company's order line and asked for a pizza to be delivered. They explained the confusion and he thanked them. Four minutes after he hung up, he received in his Inbox a list of five pizza places near him. Would *your* front-line order takers be that on the ball? Why not?

- (from the book *Christian Business Secrets*, by Ben Settle, MakeRight Publishing, Inc.) When you walk into a *Chick–fil–A*, you are entering an experience that you don't find at other fast food places. You look down at the floor and it's clean. You look at the employees and they look you in the eye and they smile at you. It's like they're all home–educated. It's like they're all intelligent. They smile at you. They're a lot smarter than I am and they're a lot happier and they're a lot more self–confident and they're not cocky. They are just what they should be;

wonderful people that are there to help you. The food is fresh and it tastes good and it's fast food, but it tastes good.

One of our neighbors recently got a job at Chick–fil–A. She's home-educated by the way. She told us about a lady who drove up with three kids in her car. It was raining and she ordered four chicken sandwiches and drinks. She paid and they gave her the drinks and then she said, "You know what? I've got these three kids. I really need to come in and eat. It's just too messy in the car. Do you mind holding my sandwiches indoors? Let me park the car and get my kids through this rain, and we're going to eat inside." The lady at the drive through, of course, said, "Yes, it would be my pleasure to have you do this." It's not like at most places where they'd go, "Huh?" She parked her car. When she got out, two employees were standing there with umbrellas to hold over those kids and that mom as they walked into the building. When she got in, all the sandwiches were there at a table and they had put napkins and eating utensils around and they helped get her three little kids there to that table from walking them in with umbrellas. Can you even *imagine* anyone else ever doing that at any fast food place? This is Customer Service *supreme*. Will that lady be the biggest evangelist for Chik-fil-A that place has ever seen? Oh yes.

How many customer evangelists for your business exist?

- Teach your customers constantly.

- Be educational in everything. Even in thank-you letters if possible. Always be helping the customer. How will your client know your USP and know that you want to provide preeminence if you don't teach them?

- Tell your customers what you are doing for them, how your product differs, and you can tell them in an "inside" way to get their attention even more fully. This is part of educating your clients and training them to look to you as preeminently.

- The higher-priced your items are, the *more* you must educate your clients.

- If you don't educate your customers, one of your competitors eventually will.

- Don't always try to close the sale, especially for returning customers of big ticket items. Help each customer make their decisions. Be their friends. Take care in them. Acknowledge them. Teach them and show you are committed to them.

- Show your clients how your product makes a difference in their lives.

- Most people look only at the generic aspects of their business: they sell shoes or real estate or insurance. Refuse to allow yourself to become a commodity. Instead, focus on your contribution to your clients' lives or business and the ultimate impact that results.

- Don't brag about what you can do; instead, tell the customer how you'll fulfill the customer's wants.

- One business sends a $20 no-strings-attached voucher to any client who does not purchase something from them within a nine-month period. If they spend $40, you probably break even on the first purchase, but of course there's a chance you'll upsell and cross sell, you once again have the chance to educate your client to your preeminence, and the client is back in the habit of coming in again.

- Send *nice* birthday cards to clients, handwritten, nothing about your business except the name, make it focus on your clients! Train sales staff to pay attention to birthdays and anniversaries and family member names and discreetly record those things when you and your staff hear them. Use their children's names when possible. Don't make it obvious you're doing this.

- Always do something for your customer when he walks in. Give him a free sample (don't say free sample, just hand him the sample and say, "Try this, I'm selling this item now and would like to know what you think of it.") If you don't have a product but a service, just do something for them, some small thing that your business can do that only takes a minute.

- If you work your attrition list and find clients who truly no longer need your product or services, don't write them off but thank them for their past loyalty and patronage and diplomatically look for quality referrals.

- Write your past customers who haven't done business with you in a while. Tell them you will shameless bribe them with an offer you lose money on if they tell you why they've left. Tell them you want their business but if you can't get it back, you want to improve so that others in the future do not face the same problems.

- Give an "early bird special" if your business has down time when customers are not likely to come to you. Perhaps two low-peak hours in a day or on a particular day.

- When answering the phone, don't ask, "Can I help you?" because you're assuming that your customer knows exactly everything you can do for them.

- Take your 20% of clients that bring in 80% of your business and take special care of them, spend more time on them, offer them better deals. Make the best use of your time and efforts this way. If you pinpoint your marketing efforts to *these* people, targeting prospects instead of suspects, you'll geometrically increase your marketing dollars.

- Once you target your 80% of income-producing clients, create incentives targeting especially for them that will attract *more* of those kinds of clients.

- Your bathrooms need to be clean of course, but go the extra mile (*especially* for service-oriented businesses) by providing: Turkish cotton washcloths, potpourri, diapers (diapers come in lots of sizes, perhaps supply the top 2 or 3 popular sizes), and so on. If customers must wait in your lobby (such as with a dentist or car repair), provide stationary and pens for note writing, notepad for note-taking, just *brainstorm* here. For example, Moms often take children to dentist and doctor so you'll more focus on notepaper for women. At auto shops or oil change locations, both men and women so consider their needs but if you grab the women in a big way here, you increase the percentage of people who would normally not come in themselves but who wait for their husbands to do it for them.

Client' Marginal Net Worth

- Learn your marginal customer income for that customer's lifetime. Randomly, select current customers and extrapolate their lifetime *profit* so you'll know how much advertising you can afford per customer.

- Your leads have specifics you should know: the cost of the lead, the conversion rate, and the residual value.

- What is the lifetime value of your next, marginal customer? *If you don't know this, you cannot know anything about how to market your product!!!!!!* Know these values and any *good* accountant can give them to you (but as a business owner, you need to understand how important it is that you recognize this and utilize this number and constantly adjust for it, make knowing this a passion):

1. How much profit in the client's first purchase?
2. How many times a year or over multi-years does the average client buy?

3. How much gross profit after the first purchase does the client spend?
4. How many years does the average client remain a client?

Know these and utilize worst-case averages to make results even better. Don't just allocate money to "advertising" or "selling expenses"! You have no basis for that. Don't figure things like, "I'm going to spend 5% of sales on advertising" or "I'll give my salesperson $XX or an XX% draw against a sale."

Knowing the "marginal net worth" of a customer *now* lets you spend what it takes to pay for that expense and maintain bottom line additions constantly. You'll know, for example, that perhaps you can give your salespeople 100% of the first sale's gross income (as long as they continue to draw the return of the same customers). This gets your sales staff excited and generates far more back-end sales once you get new clients in the door. When you know the lifetime value of your next customer, you begin to understand just how much more you can spend to get a client (or less which would be a shame because it means you've been wasting money) and you can focus better.

- Consider this more in-depth approach:

  1. Calculate your average sale and your average profit per sale,
  2. Compute how much additional profit a customer is worth to you by determining

how many times he or she comes back. Be conservative and do this assuming you really do very little (meaning whatever you normally now do) to get them to return,

3. Compute precisely how much a client costs by dividing your marketing budget by the number of clients it produces,
4. Compute the cost of a prospect the same way,
5. Compute how many sales you get for so many prospects (that's the percentage of prospects who become clients),
6. Compute the marginal net worth if a client by subtracting the cost to produce (or convert) a customer from the profit you expect to earn from a client over the lifetime of patronage.

Edited, Compiled, and Improved by Greg Perry

Competition

- If you lose too many clients to your competitors, you *must* find out what your competitors do that you don't do. Whatever they're doing, it's fantastic for them and you should get in on the action considering they *were* your customers before you failed them.

Edited, Compiled, and Improved by Greg Perry

Consultants

- Put an ad in trade journals and papers that follows this template: "Free report reveals how to keep your accounts receivables from sucking the profits out of your business. Simple, proven plan that really works! 1-800-xxx-xxxx. www.yourdomainhere.com"

Edited, Compiled, and Improved by Greg Perry

Contract Work You Need

- eLance.com is a no-brainer for most generic kinds of contract work such as commercial art, report writing, pamphlet design, and so on. Huge eLance tip: Always preface your job request with, "This is *easy* for someone who knows what they're doing."

Edited, Compiled, and Improved by Greg Perry

Costs

- With whatever you do, find out what it costs to make the items available to your business. If you resell electronics, find out what it takes to get the parts, get several quotes, and then: you have the wisdom to ask your suppliers for a better deal.

- Tax avoidance: If and when you know your marginal customer's net worth, if at the end of your taxable year, let's say you've made $400k profit and you have to pay 50% on taxes. And you may not need the money. You can take any amount up to $400K and put that into advertising and marketing (this is now a vital, capital investment because you know marketing tools that actually produce results). You then mitigate your taxes but you know the back-end and residual will make you wealthy from that amount. In that scenario, you can make this year's taxes *zero* and build *massive customers in the future that you wouldn't otherwise have*

Edited, Compiled, and Improved by Greg Perry

Coupons

- You can give every person who sees your ad a gift in the form of a coupon! This works even if you do those bathroom stall ads (ask men about these). Put the words, "Take a cell phone photo of this ad and show it the next time you come into our store for 20% off!"

- The vast majority of people respond to a coupon far faster than just a telephone number.

- You can put a *huge* coupon in your ad to make it as obvious as possible. Of course, test this to see which placement, which wording, and which size works best. (That is, if you are in a business that still warrants a yellow page ad.)

- Coupons should have dotted lines surrounding it. You don't want the reader's eyes drawn to the coupon too early because you usually want to make your offer in stages. Graphics departments tend to use too heavy of a coupon unless you tell them to lighten it up.

- Coupons should restate the action, "Yes, Sam, I want to save $923 in the next three months so my family will have more money to spend on our Christmas vacation…"

Customers

- You need to target and know your "Dream 100" clients, especially if you're a professional. You want to target Dream 100, just send reports and offers of free reports. Get your name in front of them constantly, most of your constant shouldn't even be direct selling (interspersed in-between certainly should be directly selling them).

Your Dream 100 list should contain your members of congress who live nearby, the Mayor, families of these people, company presidents, and so on. You can go to sites such as OrientalTrading.com where you can get things like flashlights and whistles by the dozens at dirt cheap prices and send one of those *every month* to your Dream 100 list, with a short letter saying something like, "Use this to Light up your business with..." or "Blow away your competitors with..." Such platitudes are a waste in traditional ads, but by providing this kind of wording, you loosely tie the item to their needs. Your only goal with this is to get your name in front of them constantly. This is one time when being kind of cute (as long as it's personal and consistent: *every* month or two) will pay off. There's no way they won't know who you are after you do this for a year.

- Preeminence: In a real sense you are stealing from your customers if you don't do your utmost to make sure you benefit your customers, make them happier, richer, more fulfilled. If you are not a preeminent business to them, you're stealing from them because you are not ensuring they have full value.

- Any time you introduce a new product or feature to a customer (or in a letter or phone call) you should always follow the introduction with, "And that benefits *you* by..." or "And that means XYZ to *you.*"

- Suppose 5 to 0% of your customers cost you more than they bring in, they always whine, they're problems. You can go to your competitors and strike a deal (or do it anonymously with a second company name) and ask, "If we send you new customers, we'd like a percentage of the first sale." You can have coupons printed and write your problem clients that says, "We don't feel we've given you the quality of service you expect. Your happiness is more important to us than our business. We've made an agreement with another company to give you a gift, a discount coupon, and we think you should see if this other company can serve you better. If so, there are no hard feelings on our part to you. If we've given you any problem, we're sincerely sorry and we want this gift to help to make up for some of the problem we've caused." This lets your competition take over your problem clients.

- In everything, keep explaining what you do. Have a "What We Do" link on your site or emails, or an "If You're New To Us" link or whatever to explain what you're all about.

- If you can get your most profitable customers to tell you the truth about why they keep buying from you, you will have a tremendous advantage in your future marketing.

- When you calibrate a customer's initial yes's and no's, you then are ready to learn their present state. Always ask things until you can get to "How did you feel when you faced this?" You are bringing them down the elevator to your sale. *Never fix anything then.* Don't offer *any* fix yet.

- Continue – Keep asking until you hear about failure and then as, "How did you feel when what you did before didn't work?," "Is this failure having any kind of impact on your friends or family?," Is there anyone else involved in this?," "Does your spouse (or business partner) object and why?" (This gets the other-person objection on the table for you to handle when you begin selling.) Your goal in learning if any third-party objection is present is to get them to a point where they say, "But I make my own decisions!"

- Continue – "What is the worst thing about this project?"

- Continue: "What are your top 3 problems to overcome to make this project a success?"

  *Ta-Da! Now you have everything you need for your sale! Make your proposal (or sales response when closing) handle those specific problems for the buyer!

- To help get more buyers on your customer list, at the point of purchase, the salesman or cashier can say, "By the way, once you buy from us, you're available to specials we only announce to existing customers, advanced sales, one-time unadvertised sales that we do not normally offer to the general public, special savings that are only available to our list. Would you mind filling out your name and address if we only use your name and address for such things?"

- Yes, they're customers but consider shifting your mindset to this: Your customers are clients not customers. It's your job to help them do or be their best, not to sell them a product or service. Preeminence!

- Do you make it easy, informative, non-threatening, and educational to do business with you and your staff? *All* your staff?

- Always tell *why*: why your price is good, why you deliver faster, why your USP is in place, tell them *Why*. Educate to give buyer more confidence.

- When you double the number of clients who do business with you, you cut in half (or more) the cost of getting new sales that you didn't otherwise have.

- Some business owe you lots of money but can't pay you? If they're not deadbeats and if they have a good mailing list, ask them to sponsor three mailings for you over the next year and give them a percentage of the business to offset what they owe you.

- For your elderly customers, have you considered driving to get them and returning them home? If you offered this, you would likely get three or four others at the same time, people who know them or live with them.

- How much is the worst-case customer's initial transaction profit? How many transactions occur per year? How many years does the average customer remain a customer? Knowing these answers will tell you a lot about what you can do. For example, you might even be able give your salespeople 100% of the first transaction's profit as a huge incentive to sell.

- Keep your eyes on the "loyalty curve" – The thing that makes customers *loyal* (not just satisfied) to your business. "They *stay* (through thick or thin), the *say* (talking to others about you, selling actively for you), and they *pay*." Keeping your current customers loyal is more vital than getting new ones. Every employee of your company needs to view themselves as problem solvers. You gain loyalty most when there's a problem. That's why your customers must view themselves as problem solvers. To do this, when the opportunity comes up and the employee misses it (the first time), get with the employee and repeat the problem and work with that employee and ask how to solve that problem in the future.

- For lost clients, offer them a free service if they'll do an exit interview with you telling you why they're moving. Make it clear that you won't try to talk them out of going elsewhere, tell them, you just want to make your business better and give them an incentive, such as a restaurant certificate, if they will give you those 15 minutes.

  This is extremely valuable. You lose customers over your business's lifetime and you have *no idea why they leave*. You must learn why people go elsewhere. Keeping customers is far easier and less costly than getting brand new customers.

- Give your customers a breakfast or a lunch. Clarify there's *no obligation* and *nothing for sale*, only the a *free lunch*. Make them the guest stars, treat them well. One of the features will be you interviewing them as you would celebrities. Learn why they buy from you, involve them don't just ask if they like you, find out *why* they buy from you. Role play, record the interview sessions if they approve, do one-on-one and full group Q&A. Be sure to ask them, "If you were telling a friend about buying our product, what would you tell them?"

- Try the fly-on-the-wall concept: What does the customer say or think right before buying your product? You can test whether or not your slogan is working if you start hearing your customers repeat it back to you.

- Know who your customer truly is. A retirement home's customer is often the children, not the elderly.

- Although this might seem to be a strange concept for any business that has nothing to do with automobiles, but consider it: Could you have an inexpensive car wash for your customers, perhaps one you don't charge for, or one you only charge enough to cover your costs? Again, think of the customer-draw this could be for completely non-automotive businesses, such as a movie theater.

- A hardware store doesn't sell shovels to people who want shovels; they sell shovels from people who want holes. So promote the ease of getting the hole they want, don't promote the features of the shovel.

Edited, Compiled, and Improved by Greg Perry

Customer Support

- Has anyone ever written an article or editorial about your product or company? Copy it on newsprint, write "Thought you may be interested in this – John,", and send it to your customer list.

- Tell your customers they may call after hours to ask questions and you'll get the answers the next day. On your voice mail, in your brochures, and when talking to a customer who hasn't made the buying decision yet, tell them to "Leave any questions on our *answering machine* (don't say *voice mail*, because even in today's modern age, that still can make some people hesitant, especially older people). Of course, your Web site should have a FAQ (Frequently Asked Questions) page for the more common inquiries you get.

- Each misstep in believability causes all other beliefs you've proved and stated to be disbelieved immediately.

- Find the top three things customers dislike most about doing business with you (anything, including your overall industry's image, you, your staff, your location, whatever). You probably do *not* already know these dislikes, even if you think you do.

  Rank these in order and you and let your employees determine how you will solve that problem and eliminate many of the dislikes from customers. This is a huge first step in becoming preeminent and developing a good USP by the way.

- Send your good customers a thank-you note. Make it hand-written and mailed. One from the salesperson and another from the owner are better than just one. Don't upsell in this note, it's to be purely an appreciation connection.

- If your customer buys for a company he works for, send your best customers' *bosses* thank-you notes. Tell them how pleasurable it was doing business with their employee. This is *huge*, helps your actual buyer a lot, and begins a longer-term relationship because the higher a person in an organization who likes you, the more business will come your way.

- Send your customers, especially the best ones, chocolate! Sean D'Souza recently wrote this in an email: "Imagine you sold a course that was worth $2500 to a client. Imagine you also sent a bar of chocolate, just as a thank you. Six years later, what does the client remember? Yes…

They remember the chocolate! Incredible as it may sound, the high expense of a course is long forgotten, but the memory of the chocolate—a single bar of chocolate—lingers on.

- Your customers need to be constantly educated of the value you are to them but you *must* do it matter-of-factly, gently, and smoothly, have your salesmen tell them what goes into it. Don't ever come across as cocky or as someone wanted accolades. You can feel good about telling your customers why they can feel good about buying from you. Bond your clients to you like epoxy.

Edited, Compiled, and Improved by Greg Perry

Doctors & Dentists

- You cannot always guarantee results, but you can guarantee satisfaction of service. You can also guarantee that the product or service performs as well or better than you described it.

- Then again… why *can't* you guarantee results? A plumber without any schooling ensures his work, you're not too good to do the same. Virtually no doctor or dentist on earth does this… Why can't you see how powerful your business would be if you were the only one who did?

- Leave the doors of the individual exam rooms open a crack as patients wait for the doctor to see them. This gives privacy but eliminates the isolated feeling that often occurs when people don't feel good.

- People associate smells to service. Make muffins or spiced tea or cider. Create a small that waiting patients can relate to that isn't medical.

Edited, Compiled, and Improved by Greg Perry

eBay

- Easy targeted traffic from eBay: If you have a website here's a way to get traffic from eBay to your website *without* policy violation: If you don't have a youtube.com account yet get one. There isn't any fee to join. When setting up your account use a domain name as your account name. For example your account name on youtube.com might be "DogLovers.com". Then, when you link to videos in your eBay auctions you'll get a lot of exposure for your site! Also "brand" your videos with your domain name in the corner. Products like Camtasia (camtasia.com) are perfect for making simple computer videos and then branding them for maximum exposure.

- If you sell eBooks or other informational products, state clearly in the eBay listing that you're the copyright owner for the item. eBay monitors this.

- Do you want more things to sell? Take out an ad in your home town newspaper that says something along the lines of, "Have stuff to sell and don't understand eBay? I'll sell your first item without any charge to show you how well my eBay auctions sell! Send email (or call)…"

eBooks

- In any eBooks you write or have written for your product or service, include this in a special note at the beginning: "As a registered user of this eBook, you're entitled to the following bonuses worth $xxx.xx: 1. ----, 2. ----, and 3. ---- (If you're reading a friend's copy, click the link below for a quick registration and access to your free bonus items."

- In a book, at the bottom of every page, put "For your free gift worth $97, send an email to: xyz@xyz.com." This builds your list rapidly.

Edited, Compiled, and Improved by Greg Perry

Email

- Spam detectors are not as sensitive when you use the person's name as the first word of the subject.

- Develop a signature tag that goes with each email you send. The signature tag should have an autoresponder report link and your Web site address.

- Always left-justify your signature tag and include the mailto: before your autoresponder email address. Keep line length under 60 characters.

- Change your signature tag regularly to see which pulls best.

- On signup link to your newsletter, ask only for their email address. Second screen after they click they want to sign up for free newsletter, ask: Do you mind giving us your first and last name so we can personalize your reports. Also, select whether they'd prefer to have regular ASCII text or colorful HTML emailed reports.

- Snail mail has a 2,000% to 12,000% higher
  believability factor than email. But you often
  start with email. Get your regular email list and
  mail physically to it once in a while with a big
  offer.

- In email, keep all lines under 60 characters long.
  Use a hard return at the end of each line. Use a
  fixed-character font such as Courier New. Save
  as a .TXT file. Use plenty of compelling
  subheadings.

- Offering many more email tips would just be
  senseless. The best overall tip I can give you is
  to go to EmailPlayers.com and sign up for the
  emailed daily tips but for the power you want,
  get the amazing newsletter. Please note, I get
  nothing for referring you to this newsletter. The
  newsletter isn't free because that would be
  foolish for such jam-packed issues of
  information on how you can skyrocket your
  business success with the simple use of emails.

Employees

- Make sure your employees are paid on a performance basis as much as possible.

- You will need to train, realign, and continually calibrate your employees to maintain a preeminence with your clients. Make sure your front-line employees maintain this.

- To keep happiness within your company, hire slowly and fire quickly.

- Make your staff celebrities! Have your staff write sales letters saying, "The Boss doesn't know what he's doing… he gave *us* the job of marketing and we don't know what we're doing, but neither does he!" This is great for doctors and dentist. Make fun of the staff, and the more serious and professional a staff person is, the more hokey he or she should be in the newsletter. The staff will love being local celebrities!

Stan Lee did this at *Marvel Comics* during the 60s and 70s. Readers thought the "Marvel Bullpen"

– the onsite staff – was massive and they were always cutting up, joking, having a great time. The reality is that the offices had virtually no people because most of the writers and artists worked from other cities and towns. Stan Lee was just making up most of it but it created a reality in the readers' minds that there was a constant party going on at all times at Marvel. Stan gave them all nicknames and everywhere an artist's name appeared, his nickname would appear. In the back of each comic was a message from Stan telling about the latest antics in the Marvel Bullpen. That one tactic was responsible for *almost* putting Marvel's Distinguished Competitor (DC Comics) out of business.

- If you motivate employees with incentives, and you should, then consider putting into place incentives for teams, not for individuals except for obvious exceptions. Home Depot offers no individual incentives because their employees will sell customers products and not true solutions to customer problems.

- A good employee incentive profit-sharing plan is to base their bonus on actual profit so take 10% (or whatever) and if your company makes $1,000 you divide the 10% based on a pro-rated salary percentage within the company. So a higher-salaried employee gets a higher bonus but the bonus is not based on their salary but on profit.

- Reward an "ABC Employee:" – Above, Beyond the Call of Duty!

- Don't have huge prize for highest sales manager or "Most XX Employee!" because it creates resentment and the one who wins it would have won it anyway. Have smaller and more numerous incentives like 100 employees $10 instead of one $10,000, or create ranges of incentives like from $10 to $45 and the ones who get $45 are few and far between.

- Acknowledge every incentive that is reasonable, acknowledge with a voucher or handshake or visit from the highest person in your company.

- The highest person in the company is the one who should monitor suggestions from the employee suggestion box. With those suggestions, it dramatically reduces grumbling among the ranks if employees see reasonable suggestions being implemented. They will work with you and not just for you. You can take the top suggestions like the one who won the most $45 prizes and give them an extra bonus or 2-day vacation or whatever. This kind of top prize is still very available to other employees and they won't feel the resentment.

- Have weekly meetings with your staff to improve your company. Discuss "what are our top 3 ways to solve this problem, sell this product, improve our service?" Take notes in that meeting. At the end of the year, you have 52-weeks' worth of notes that you can publish into a pamphlet entitled, "52 Ways We've

Improved Our Company This Year" that you
can send to clients along an offer of some kind.

- How many times have you walked into your
  business as a customer (perhaps disguised) and
  saw things from a customer's standpoint? How
  many times have you done the same for your
  competitors? Shouldn't you do this often?
  Shouldn't you send your own staff to do the
  same at both places to learn and to teach you
  what they found?

- Your staff needs to have targeted titles. Not
  "brokers," for example, but "precious metals
  specialists."

- On a retreat, gather your employees together
  with someone (perhaps a customer or two and
  an industry expert) who will describe all the
  horrors of doing business with either you or
  your industry. Then problem-solve the top
  three solutions together.

Endorsements

- Endorsements should be specific, perhaps the endorser can tell why you saved money or delivered faster. If it's a client who has a mailing list, let the client offer a free product or service to his or her clients that you give. In other words, perhaps the endorser says that his clients can have a free hour of your service without strings attached because he thinks so much of you. Then, your endorser certainly could get a percentage of any *subsequent* business his clients give you after that initial freebie.

- You can even get a competitor to endorse you. Go to your competitor and ask if he will introduce his lost customer to you saying something like, "I know you've gone elsewhere and I respect that. I don't take it personally. I'd love to have your business back and I'll do whatever I can to get it. But in case you still want to look elsewhere, I'd like to recommend a friend and, yes, a competitor, whom I respect enough to tell you about." Then, you can even give that competitor 100% of the first sale if you have back-end or multi-purchase customers generally. This costs you nothing in advertising, yet you get a new customer. If you advertised, you'd be paying for that customer, so giving the sale's profit to your competition isn't a real loss.

Ezines, Blogs, and Web Articles

- In writing a blog or "ezine" article or even a regular sales letter, consider lists: "10 Easy Ways to ...," "Top 10 Hottest ...," "5 Tips to determine if your Pest Control guy is doing his job," "7 steps to growing better roses..."

- An article or autoresponder report is often effective when it's a tutorial, step-by-step tutorial or a checklist with things to look out for.

- Use opinion in newsletters, blog articles, and ezines. The most engaged readers prefer bias.

- Autoresponders, such as Aweber.com, are gold for many businesses, yet only a few are aware of their existence and how to use them.

- If you put a different autoresponder code on each web page of your site (the major pages) you learn quickly which pages are most effective and most visited.

Edited, Compiled, and Improved by Greg Perry

Face-to-Face Selling

- When selling, find out the customer's actual criteria. Ask questions such as, "What would be your number one goal if you could have any goal for this [project/item/whatever you are selling]?" and then keep asking deeper and deeper until you get to some core desires. Then you start selling them by *playing back their criteria and you offer features!* If you sell cars but their criteria is safety for children, you focus on the safety factors in a major way.

Edited, Compiled, and Improved by Greg Perry

Failure

- Do *not* allow yourself to see any result as a failure. For example, if you can't get people to take your surveys, find out *why* they won't. If you can't turn leads into closes, find out *why* you can't. If your competition is outselling you, find out *why*. Be creative, resourceful, and ask lots of questions to learn the answer to the *why*'s.

- When you tell your customers what you can do, tell them *why*. Why you can deliver better, why your price is better, why you can offer more bonuses, and so on.

- If you don't make money online, don't blame the Internet. It's just a numbers game. There is something… A wrong target audience, your sales letter, price, testing,… there's something you don't know. Often it's a headline or lead-generation problem.

- If you don't get No's you cannot repair every little thing that you're doing wrong. Feedback and adjustment are vital and should continue through the life of your business.

Follow-Ups

- Always follow-up sales letters, customer inquiries, and your current and past customer list with calls.

- Rapid response is best response. Three words that perform magic when a customer asks for something are: "Sure, right away!" Say it positively without over-exaggerating and you will seal trust instantly (of course you must follow up in a quick manner, or you will lose far more trust than you gained).

- Grow your business each year by sending out questionnaires to former and current customers. This works for high cost, low volume businesses like window installations. Such a business sends out a questionnaire every 1, 5, and 10 years. Clients respond with "The still look good!" and all that. But you have put your business in front of those customers and if they move and need windows or (more important) if they talk to others about your windows, you have powerful word of mouth advertising.

- Be educational in everything. Even in thank-you letters if possible. Always be helping the customer.

- *Always* follow up actual sales with a call, email, or letter. This helps alleviates buyer's remorse, enables you to handle any possible problems, upsell, and simply make better contact and an impression on your clients.

- When writing notes, sending cards, or acknowledging thank-you's from customers, never ever make your handwriting look rushed or sound cookie-cutter. Make each unique and targeted to your customer.

- Give a free seminar to an association and collect business cards for a special report. Then follow-up by sending that free report with an aurtoresponder, and then call later call them.

- Always have a regular, follow-up contact strategy for all new clients no matter what your business is, although for ones such as car lots, this may be a fairly long time between clients. Of course, for those kinds of things you look to other complementary businesses, such as a car wash and detailing, that you can refer to for your "special clients," but that you also get referral fees and a shared customer list.

- Use the phone for follow-up if your business is geared that way (not all online). Call once the customer orders from a mailing or online and say you're making sure the customer found everything okay. And because they bought, you'll keep an approved offer open for a while "but please, don't feel any obligation, we're just pleased that you are pleased and we want to be here if you ever need anything else."

- Every once in a while, write a personal letter (you can type it but make sure you sign it, and possibly hand address it) to describe in deep detail an expensive new product or service you have.

- Once you follow-up... follow-up once again. Then again. But each time, offer a special service or value and not just a sales call. Say, "Oh, let me email you more information."

- Your follow-up letter doesn't have to be just a reminder, it can be and should be something such as news about a new service or product and how they can get a special deal as a current customer. Time this to be about the time when they'd normally be thinking about returning anyway. Test which kind of follow-up works. For example, perhaps a CD or USB stick may do the job for some things, perhaps a FedEx of a sample or whatever. Make it provide immediate value to your client just to get the follow-up and then tell them an action.

- Don't use mailing labels. Either laser print your addressee directly onto the envelope or handwrite (best for small businesses and salesman letters and birthday cards, etc.) the address.

- Call your customer after a sale to see if things went smoothly. If they didn't you'll know about it anyway! So it's better to call first and do what you can to fix the problem. If not, then make sure the customer is happy and say you're glad and to enjoy. And then possibly upsell, possibly tell about a quantity discount if they might buy again, or perhaps (you must decide which is most appropriate) don't do an upsell at that point.

Freebies

- Any time you think about licensing a product for others to sell, make it cheap if it's the kind of thing someone can easily copy and give away anyway.

Edited, Compiled, and Improved by Greg Perry

Free Reports

- "Claim your free report" is more effective than "Get" or "Receive."

- Sometimes you must have a sales letter for a free report or autoresponder item since people are bombarded with too much info these days and tired of junk email.

- Before distributing a Report in Word format, be sure to clean the revision marks and document properties of anything you want hidden.

- When distributing PDF documents, consider using some of the PDF security tools to keep the document from being changed and passed on.

Edited, Compiled, and Improved by Greg Perry

Front-End

- Front-end products *must* over deliver in quality and expectations.

- A day after you sell a front-end product, send an email asking if the customer received the product and if everything works fine. in addition, send another freebie to make the sale stick. Word it, "You won't find anything being sold here, just my offer to help if things didn't go smoothly. And here's a gift of thanks for you, a free bonus for your time." (This could be an informational report or a coupon for a free item in your business.)

- Offer first-time clients product or service at cost (half off or whatever). Empires grow to larger empires because they have repeat business, add-ons, and back-end products.

- Are you selling a front-end product with a low margin hoping for the large, high-margin back-end sale? *Consider* selling only your back-end item and giving away your front-end.

- Give a free trial, a courtesy evaluation, one-half salesman commission, double warranty period, do whatever small costs to bring more initial sales to your door. Buy customers at break-even or a loss for the first, front-end sale. A large front-end loss is easily possible if your customer's lifetime conversion value on the back end is successful.

Fund-Raising

- If you give them readers multi-priced options to check, such as you might do on a charity-giving card, go from high to low. Then they feel good that there are people below them and it helps. If you are testing only, do the opposite from low to high and test each combination.

- Fund-raising has to work on emotion. It's a little disingenuous. You usually don't offer something for the money so to be successful, offer a premium for a donation.

- Most fund-raising doesn't really tell the full story about what the organization does and what will be done with the money. Also, a money-back guarantee for donations are hardly *ever* done but are *very* powerful incentives!

- *Recency* is the case where a person who recently bought from you is more likely to buy again sooner than someone else will. Often charities use recency to send donation requests to people who just gave to them.

You must use wisdom in determining your recency list. Let's say you're selling a video program titled "Overcoming Infertility: How to Have a Child When You've Been Trying Without Success." The price is $99. You rent a list of people who have subscribed to an infertility magazine for $12. You mail to the list, and the mailing doesn't pull.

Why not?

The problem is this: While the people on the list have demonstrated (a) an interest in infertility and (b) that they buy information by mail, they have *not* demonstrated that they will spend $99 on a mail-order product. $12, sure; $99, no.

The solution? Find a list of people who have attended a workshop on infertility or bought a test kit via mail-order for $100 or more.

General & Miscellaneous

- Don't be stuck to making money *your* way. Be open to change if that change is to benefit your customers more.

- Your business is marketing to your customers. Your business is not your product. Your product should be your area of expertise.

- What is your level of client attrition? Most businesses don't know. Attrition is the number of clients who stop doing business with you or your enterprise. They move, they get unhappy, they get lazy, they go somewhere else. These are the clients *you* failed to show preeminence to.

- A monthly special would be a good idea.

- Three ways to increase business: 1. Get more clients, 2. Increase sale per client, and 3. Increase the client return rate. Do any two and your business grows geometrically. Do all three and your business grows exponentially.

- People don't buy products, they buy solutions. All of your marketing is to provide a solution.

- Questions for that aid business analysis:

- Where do my clients come from specifically (the demographics)?

- Would I rather attract new clients or garner more from current clients and why?

- Who else benefits from my success (besides clients, my employees, my family)?

- How many supplies/businesses would be motivated to help me grow my business more because it will directly benefit them at a high level? Who are they?

- When I create a new client for my business, who else am I creating a client for?

- What is the biggest client complaint about my company and what do I to address that?

- Who are my biggest competitors and what do they offer that I do not?

- What is my competitor's biggest failing and how could I specifically fill that void?

- What is my biggest and best source of new business and what am I doing to obtain that new business?

- What has been my biggest marketing effort to date?

- What is my biggest marketing problem?

- What better ways exist that will enable me to reduce the barriers of entry for new clients, or reduce the hurdle for my clients to make it easier to do business with me?

- Do I have a large supply of client testimonials?

- What can I do to obtain more testimonials?

- What do I do to actively solicit referral business?

- In what ways do I up-sell my clients?

- How does my guarantee or warranty compare to my competition's?

- What would happen to my business if I took a one-month vacation? Are my employees grounded enough in my USP that things can continue as usual?

- Which activity does my business do that takes the most work and brings the least return? How can I begin to eliminate or lessen that activity?

- Which activity does my business do that takes the *least* work and brings the most return? How can I begin to increase that activity?

- Is there anyone who could run your business as well or better than you? If you hired them, would you still make a profit? If not, what would you have to do to answer "yes" to this?

- Ask yourself, "Who stands to benefit if I make higher sales?"

- Ask yourself, "What other ways can I benefit from the goodwill of my clients?"

- Ask yourself, "What better ways can I reduce the risk of my transactions to get more clients and keep the ones I have coming back?"

- Locate the best source of new business (geographically and every other way). Go deeper, don't just say "referral sales are our best income" but go deeper to find out what you do and why you do it to get those referrals. Go deeper to get specific.

- The best way of dealing with "We don't do that" is to ask yourself/your employees/your customers: "But if we did, how could it work?"

- Watch what clients do after buying from you. Do they go to another business for a complementary product? If so, why can't you offer that product, or create a joint-venture with that company, to promote their products with a special?

- "Marketing genius" is not creative ingenuity. It's getting the maximum result from your efforts and knowing which efforts produce the most results and sticking to them.

- Find out why your top 20% clients bring in 80% of your business and duplicate it as much as possible. Find out where it's coming from and where if could come from.

- Marketing is not a one-step process (getting customer in door). When you use 2-step, you develop preeminence in the customer's thoughts and minds and when they come to you it's like they've made up their mind. It's not a cold lead but one who is very interested in doing business with you.

Edited, Compiled, and Improved by Greg Perry

Google AdWords and Pay Per Click Advertising

- Surprisingly, positions 3, 4, and 5 often outsell Google positions 1 & 2. But test this for *your* business.

Edited, Compiled, and Improved by Greg Perry

Grocery Stores

- No business is immune from the power of direct marketing. Grocery stores can do everything just as business-to-business and traditional retailers and online businesses.

- For a grocer, give samples. The fact that Sam's lines its aisles every weekend with sample providers is not a coincidence. Sam's does nothing for long that doesn't add to their return.

- Be your customers' preeminent grocery solution. Run ads that show you're a kitchen solution store. Send handwritten thank-you letters to good customers. Make sure your employees are friends to your customers. Provide free, high quality coffee (make sure you sell this coffee right at that point of sampling too.)

- Include package inserts in shopping bags like booklets with little note showing you going the extra mile without any bragging, just sincerity. Tell shoppers that they can call at any time with questions about products. Write about upcoming sales, collect addresses and phone numbers during drawings for items. Add bag stuffers and show that you are concerned about them. Include questionnaires once in a while asking shoppers which items they wish you sold and give them a coupon for returning the questionnaire (or by filling it out online); never make the questionnaire long, always short to respect their time. Put safety information in the bag. Be charming to your customers and make sure your employees are also! Ask for feedback in a comments box and collect names and emails for any replies or follow up (for your lists).

Guarantee

- If you don't offer a 100% guarantee, but you accept credit cards and PayPal for payments, then you unwittingly *do* offer a 100% money-back guarantee and it's a far more dangerous guarantee than offering the money-back refund in your sales material.

  Because if you mess up, or if your customers think you did, and you don't handle the problem to their satisfaction, when you tell them you don't refund purchases, they'll immediately dispute the charge on their credit card or through PayPal. On such disputes, the buyer almost *always* wins.

  The bottom line to such disputes is that your buyer will almost *always* get his money back, your credit card processor will consider that a strike against keeping you as a client, and you lost sales originally because some buyers look for that guarantee to consider you trustworthy. Many customers who know nothing about you or your product or service will never buy because the risk is all on them.

- A successful company always puts the buying risk on themselves, never their customers.

- A good guarantee for service clients: if you don't like what we've done, we'll redo it. If you still don't like what we've done, you pay us nothing.

- "Try it out, full refund if you don't like it." No hassle, don't decide now to keep it, give it a try first. No hard feelings.

- Here is a fabulous guarantee, more effective than "Lifetime Guarantee": "Guaranteed for One Million Years! (Or: Guaranteed for My Lifetime… and I'm Healthy!")

- Make sure that your product/service is *exactly* the way you present it. Then, if it's a very subjective issue whether or not the product/service does as you describe and they still want a refund, you can qualify it some, such as, "As long as you give this an effort to produce the results I promise," or whatever. Make sure they know that what you want to do is remove all risk from their decision.

- Offer a 1-year money-back guarantee, even if you want your money back at 11:50pm on the 365th day.

Hair Salons & Barbershops

- Consider postcards that their haircut is due, offer discount on product if they bring in the card.

- Sell ad-on products. But believe in them, or get better products. Use those products on customers.

- Make deals with other vendors your customers might do business with (hair supply stores) so both of you can give coupons for doing business with each other.

- So many customers (especially men) wait until their hair gets raggedy and then calls for an appointment and has to wait a few days to get in. Ethically train your clients that you will be in charge of reminding them about a regular visit that you schedule. Make it a service because you want them to look their best and also by doing this, each appointment will look better because their hair will be more consistent.

- For hair solons and barbershops: Teach your employees how to tell customers, "Do you really want to look attractive? It's just my personal opinion to schedule you in every X weeks given your style, etc. You'd look good continuously and not have the final week or two looking a little off. If it's okay, I will schedule your next appointment and I'll send a postcard or text a few days before..." If you want to do this, you'd feel better, you'd look better, and it would help my scheduling also so I could give you a discount each time you do this, say 15%.

- Have you thought of rewarding your great customers with a free haircut once in a while? Out of the blue. Just because we appreciate your business, don't charge your better customers. (It's best to do this privately where other customers being served don't hear you doing this.)

- Do you offer free cutting of bangs (or any kind of touch-up) between style appointments if they drop in? Why not, you want to differentiate yourself from all the other competitors, don't you? Do you teach your customers how to do their own hair each day (always educate them with your own grooming brushes, combs, and hair products)? Do you show customers what more they could do if they bought a good brush from you once you show them the "*best way* to use it"? Do you have a link to a product source, such as Aveda, and you concentrate on teaching your customers about that product line as you use it? Do you have a code of conduct on how well the customer needs to look before you allow that customer out the door?

Your competitors do none of this either. But the first one that begins will drive all hair clients to them from you. So why don't *you* be the one who does all this instead of somebody else?

Edited, Compiled, and Improved by Greg Perry

Headlines

- Often, if you put open and closing quote marks around your headlines, it outsells. People love to read quotes.

- Make your headline larger and bolder than the rest of the text. If you don't, it doesn't pull them in. If it's as powerful as it should be, then you want them to see it first.

- According to Dan Kennedy, for stronger headlines:

  1. Telegraph a dynamic benefit or promise,
  2. Add "How to" to the beginning,
  3. "Flag" your targeted prospects (Example: "Arthritis Sufferers: How to end pain in 59 seconds"),
  4. Arouse Curiosity,
  5. Use meaningful specifics (i.e. "59 seconds" is more specific than "in seconds"),
  6. Use powerful attention-grabbing words like "Warning," "Guaranteed," "New," and "Now."

- Triplets are great in headlines, such as "Get Good, Get Fast, and Get Paid!" Also, such triplets all throughout are effective.

- Read your headline out loud. Then your ad's copy. As you do, ask "So what?" or "Why cares?" after any paragraph, toss out the paragraph or edit it. Obviously, do the same for your headline and sub-heads.

- If you compete on price, a good headline is "A <*Product name's*> Revenge…" and then say it's because your competitors are all selling this for six times what you're selling it for.

- Use words in headline like *Propel, Ignite,* and *Expel.* These words show expulsion of your emotion. Use a thesaurus to find incredible words, look through your sales letter when you're done with it, and re-scan it with a thesaurus throughout.

- Keep headline long enough to motivate reader to take next step but not so long that he can't read it in 5 seconds. Prefer 25 words or fewer, but this isn't an ironclad rule.

- Generally, it's a bad idea to put the product name in headline.

- Dan Kennedy's Acid Headline Test - Separate the headline from everything else, out of context, and treat it like a classified ad… does it work on its own?

- "Free Information Kit …," "New Report Shows…" These are good headlines. Don't rely on curiosity or your product, but rather, clearly show a benefit.

- "At Last…" is a great start of a headline. Also, "Discover the…" and "A New Way to…"

- These are good words: *method, plan, reveals, simple, advanced*, and *improved.*

- Use *YOU* a lot, even in all caps.

- Your headline can't really be too long, although the general rule is to make it as long as needed without one more word, and as short as needed without one less word. The message is what's important.

- "I'm going to *explode* if I don't get this off my chest!" or "I've got to get this off my chest before I *explode!*" A sub-headline to that could be: "Why almost everybody is wrong in the way they look at XYZ." "Essential Information," Incredible Benefits," and "Call Now."

- Target who you want to reach, i.e., "If you are over 45…"

- "We sell more XXX than XXX because we sell them for $XXX less."

- "Free Report Reveals All the Secrets Landlords need…"

- Great headline: "Here's What Really Bugs Me about…"

- Great headline: With <blank>, You'll Finally Be Able to <Blank>

- Most headlines do *not* answer, "What's in it for me?" That's why most headlines are a waste.

- Analyze what you currently do so you'll know where you are underperforming. It may be your sales staff, your prospect grabbers, your lead generators, your barrier of entry, lack of risk reversal, a bad headline (or worse...*no* headline).

  For example, if you currently run an ad, and it works fairly well, then have you tested changing the headline to leverage the ad's power? No downside risk (the ad still costs the same) and total upside. The headline should be the first and primary result of your product or service.

- Be specific! Promise: How, Why, Things, Which, Which of these, Who, Who Else"

- Good for sales letter headline according to Gary North: 3-line, 18-point boldface type.

- Good Headline: "When I saw how much I saved, my jaw almost dropped to the ground!"

- Great for headlines or sub-heads: "What to do when bad things happen..."

- A headline should usually pass the Dan Kennedy "Stand Alone Test" - For example, "This is what Doctors do when they have back pain! For free information: 1-800-..." - Very few headlines pass this test, some cannot. But if yours can, it'll be far more effective.

- Not general such as "Make Money Now," but specific such as "Pay Next Month's Rent With…"

- One great headline: "Looking for $190 worth of XX for $67? We have 102 in stock right now!"

- Use rare talk like, "goof," "feel rotten," "pot-belly," and "Don't belly ache if you keep on…" so that you use terminology that is not typical and hardly ever seen in ads.

- As stated above, try enclosing headlines in quotes. If you have a header lead in, then a headline, then a sub-headline, put quotes at the beginning of the header, at the beginning of the headline, and at the beginning of the sub-head, and don't close them until the sub-headline is finished. (Proper grammar says don't put end quotes on a multi-paragraph quote until the final one.)

- Questions are powerful headlines that almost force people to read the copy.

- "Five Familiar XYZ Troubles - Which do You Want to Overcome?"

- "Discover Your…"

- Here's the real power of headlines: "I bet that I can write a newspaper page full of solid type and you'll read every word of it once you read me headline!" "Bet you can't!" says Jim Smith. "I'll prove it, look at it: 'This page is all about Jim Smith!'"

- Risk of loss is more powerful than possible gain. "A little mistake cost a farmer $7,200 a year" is better than, "Make $7,200 a year more"

- People want advice (although they don't always follow it) so, "Advice To XYZ-Group…" and "Advice" is a good headline word.

- "Who Else Wants a/to XYZ?" - Here the "else" is powerful because it shows that the deed already works.

- "Do you make these mistakes when you XYZ?" - Here, "These" is powerful and promises to teach and not just give ad fluff.

- The undiscovered angle is wonderful: "Thousands have XYZ - But Never Discovered it!"

- "How to…" ads, if they teach in the copy, are often cut out and saved to be reread and passed along!

- "This almost-magical XYZ…" the "almost" lends credibility.

- Before-and-After is good: "I Used to *Hate* being a landlord!"

- "Throw Away Your XYZ!" is great when your product or service eliminates an annoyance.

- Negative headlines like, "If you've already paid your homeowners this year, don't read this ad" usually do *not* work well. Something like, "Don't do A until you read this free report" is better.

"Don't read this headline" ads usually don't produce good results.

- A headline is to sell the ad! Solve a problem! Turn the customer's problem into a headline! For example: Suppose your product/service is Web design services. Problem: People hire freelancers but projects aren't completed on time. Surveys tell you this is a problem to most people. Your headline would then be: "Tired of graphic designers who can't keep deadlines? We meet your deadlines."

- John Caples's 5 Rules for Writing Headlines:

  1. Put the reader's self-interest into *every* headline.
  2. If you have news, such as a new product or new way to use your product, put that in your headline.
  3. Avoid headlines that only provoke curiosity – unless you can combine that with #1 and #2.
  4. Suggest there is a quick and easy way to get what the reader wants.
  5. Try to avoid gloomy headlines – there are exceptions.

- Here's a golden list of sales letter, headline, and ad magical words (NLP theory often uses these): Absolutely.. Action.. Amazing.. Approved.. Attractive.. Authentic.. Bargain...Beautiful.. Better.. Big.. Bonus.. Colorful.. Colossal.. Complete.. Confidential.. Controversial... Crammed.. Delivered.. Direct.. Discount.. Easily.. Endorsed.. Enormous..

Essential.. Excellent.. Exciting.. Exclusive..
Expert.. Explosive.. Extraordinary.. Extreme...
Famous.. Fascinating.. Fortune.. Free.. Full..
Genuine.. Gift.. Gigantic.. Greatest..
Guaranteed.. Helpful.. Highest.. Huge..
Immediately.. Immense.. Improved..
Incredible.. Informative.. Instructive.. Intense..
Interesting.. Largest.. Latest.. Lavishly.. Liberal..
Lifetime.. Limited.. Love.. Lowest.. Lucky..
Magic.. Mammoth.. Mega... Miracle.. New..
Noted.. Odd.. Outstanding.. Personalized..
Popular.. Powerful.. Practical.. Professional..
Profitable.. Profusely.. Proven.. Quality..
Quickly.. Rare.. Reduced.. Refundable..
Remarkable.. Reliable.. Revealing..
Revolutionary.. Scarce.. Secrets.. Secure..
Security.. Selected.. Sense.. Sensational..
Simplified.. Sizable.. Special.. Startling.. Strange..
Strong.. Sturdy.. Suave.. Successful.. Superior..
Surprise.. Terrific.. Tested.. Tremendous..
Undeniably.. Unconditional.. Unique..
Unlimited.. Unparalleled.. Unsurpassed..
Unusual.. Useful.. Valuable.. Warm.. Wealth..
Weird.. Wonderful…

- In your headline, you can associate with people
  ("9 of our 10 decorators use...") or use a
  dichotomy ("How I Learned to cut hair from a
  bald barber,") or "Here's what you can do
  to…" Also, tie authority to claims, such as
  "Here's what doctors do when they feel
  rotten…" Use before and after claims such as,
  "Before XXX, hay fever medication made you
  drowsy." Address those who can't buy such as,
  "If You've Already Taken Your Vacation this

year don't read this because it'll break your
heart!"

Edited, Compiled, and Improved by Greg Perry

Host/Beneficiary Relationships

- There's no strain to create powerfully profitable host-beneficiary relationships. This is all you need to do:

  1. Ask yourself, "Who already has a strong relationship with people to whom I might be able to sell a noncompetitive but related product or service?"

  2. Once you've got names on paper, contact those noncompeting businesses and ask them to introduce your product or service to their audience. Supply them with plenty of information on what you sell, and some testimonials attesting to its high quality.

- Locate companies that have clients logically predisposed to your product or service (for example, a real estate company might have clients interested in a carpet cleaner; a stockbroker might have clients interested in a financial planner.) Negotiate with those companies to sell your product or service to their clients and each company should give an endorsement to your product or service, and in return they should receive a certain percentage of the profits from all sales or another form of compensation like donations to their favorite charity or help with their accounting expenses.

- Be creative when asking the host for the deal. Don't say, "This can make you a free $50,000," but say, "This can buy your wife a new Lexus this year."

- Be sure to let the person know this will not take away from current business (and be sure you design it so that it does not).

- To develop a host-beneficiary relationship, you can *easily* go to people who sell complimentary products and say, "If we bring you customers at absolutely no marketing costs to you, and you can keep all the back end after the initial sale, would you give us 25% of the initial sale/service?"

Jay Abraham's Methods from "Getting Everything You Can Out of All You've Got"

- His book that is perfect for advertising newcomers

- Maximize what you have. Jay's techniques are some of the only techniques that provide UPside leverage only.

- Assess your current business strengths through Q&A's to discover your USP.

- The Strategy of preeminence:

  1. Educate your clients constantly
  2. Calculate the lifetime value of a client
  3. Eliminate all buyer risk. You'll have to evaluate all client hesitations to purchase to find all the reasons for purchase hesitation.
  4. Test, test, and test, and never stop testing.
  5. Develop referral programs
  6. Develop host-beneficiary relationships
  7. Reconnect with past clients

8. Make sales letters direct sales.
9. Concentrate on 20% biggest clients/ads/things-that-work.
10. Telemarket cold only as follow-up after mailing and/or client contact

Joint Ventures

- JV's are great when you're just starting out without a list.

- You can send sales letters for joint ventures. Send it to someone with a list for example. You can afford to send it FedEx, include funny $1 million dollar bills, send a special gift, or whatever. You want them to call you ("Make enough free money to pay your mortgage without doing one single extra thing.")

- You need to do all the joint venture work when you are getting the list. They are too busy with whatever they're doing. And part of the benefit to them is you'll do all the work.

- Once you get a huge list, you can send sales letters for others to joint venture products with you but then they do all the work, etc.

Edited, Compiled, and Improved by Greg Perry

List

- The money is in your list.

- One way to obtain lists is by looking under "mailing lists" in your yellow pages in big cities for any local mailings you want to do, and of course on the Internet for national mailings. These kinds of lists are broken down and sorted and available by many categories. Also, these two national companies supply them: R. L. Polk & Company at (404) 447-1280 or Donnelly List Marketing at (203) 353-7385.

- Build your list, work your list, your list is crucial. Offer freebies, offer bonuses. Get people to opt in. Use drop-in opt-in code on your site. Keep your newsletter under 65 characters wide. Confirm the opt-in with an email and keep the opt-in email as proof you are not spamming. If you ask for the subscriber's first name or zip code, this serves as proof of the opt-in. otherwise, you can have them reply to a confirmation email but this is often a hassle for the client. The double opt-in option is less problematic than it was a few years ago, however, because far more customers are used to the process.

- On the first screen or pop-up of any site's free report, ask only for their email address. The next screen they see they click that they want to sign up for a free newsletter (or book or report), always ask: "Do you mind giving us your first and last name so we can personalize your reports?" On that second screen, have a link to your home page and also they go to the home page if they answer the questions and click the button.

- How often do you contact the top ten on your client list and call them to tell them how grateful you are for their business? You then can send them a follow-up letter in a week giving them a special deal that beats what they would normally be buying from you anyway about that time.

- Try this to see how well it pulls: On your web site where you do an opt-in, on the first screen for a free report or whatever offer you're giving them for the sign up, ask only for email address. On a *second* screen after they click they want to sign up for your free newsletter or offer, then ask something along the lines of: "Do you mind giving us your first and last name so we can personalize your report? Also, select below whether you'd prefer to have regular ASCII text or colorful HTML emailed reports." On that second screen, have a link to your home page, but also take them to your home page if they answer the questions and click the button.

- Have a Guestbook in your store! Ask for emails as well as physical addresses!

- Don't have lists? Rent one. Rent several. Target people who want or need your products and services.

- Be creative. Perhaps send an invitation for your new business to dentists and tell them this month you're giving a free XXX for every dentist who comes in. If they ask you why when they come in, you will tell them. (Have a plausible reason.) Then do it for other professions/categories if that works. You can even do this by certain kinds of car owners ("Mustang Day" or whatever.) Also, "List Brokers" can help with very specific lists.

- Your customer lists *do* contain customer's hobbies and likes and dislikes when you can get this information easily without prying, right? So you can begin to target better direct sales letters to them?

- Get your list - then sell to it over and over and over.

- Need to rent mailing targeted lists? Go to www.edithroman.com or access lists online through srds.com

- If you've developed a list of product buyers in your field, and if you have not, you need to now, go to www.edithroman.com and offer your list for rent and you'll make a fee each time another company uses it. If the site is down you can go to the library to look in Direct Mail Rates and Data Book to do the same thing. Make sure you don't rent a list of customers whom you've promised never to share.

- Don't use bulk mail because contacts don't get your mail if they move due to no forwarding. Also, it's not personal and often not opened. Use a first class stamp and just a simple, regular return address. Put a real letter inside, if the client opens your envelope and sees immediately it's an ad it could go in the trash. Once tested, try with bulk to see if the less response is worth saving the postage costs.

- Don't cold sell with untargeted lists or single calls. Get referrals from others, get them to sell your product.

- If you have a great mailing list and want to do something in addition to back-ending it, you should broker it out but you will reap more benefit if you do a host-beneficiary relationship where company B uses your list and you get a percentage of sales from that. If you are protective of your list, you can "bond" your list with a list company/broker so the list doesn't actually get into the hands of the other company but the list bonder does the mailing.

- When you rent a mailing list, it's common to take the Nth number of names (5th or so) to get a random sample but there are devious mailing list brokers. If you are new, it's a much better test if you get a complete geographical region like all of L.A., or take two or three complete geographical regions and see how well they do. This is more accurate to test the broker than just every nth name.

- When you own a list that you rent to others, put phony names on addresses that you own somewhere and if those addresses get sent things more times than the list was rented, then you know the list renter abused the list.

- Test this but often when sending mailings to companies, you get a better response when you put only the company name instead of a specific person. Even better, a department or a vague title that several people might have.

Mail

- Window envelopes can out-pull blank or envelopes on the outside. Even if you use mailing labels, the window envelope gets read more often. You have a max of 4 seconds to get their attention. Consider how the letter is folded and what they see first. They usually don't even pull out the letter all the way before discarding it. You have a max of 4 seconds to grab them.

- Print in a handwritten font on the outside of an envelope: "Your tickets are enclosed!" to almost guarantee an opening of the envelope.

- On the envelope, do you put a bunch of stuff on the outside (Look inside, look here, ses-through, handwritten address, stamp, whatever)? As always for such things, you won't know what works best until you test. And you must continually test.

- A direct mail letter on yellow (goldenrod is better) can be quite effective and should be tested for those who mail.

- Hardly anybody copies successful direct mail techniques. Why? Shouldn't *you* begin doing it if your competitors won't? (And they won't). Copy techniques, never words. If you only copy words, not only are you stealing from the original writer, but you're stealing from yourself by not writing the most effective sales letter you can write for your *own* products and services. Copying words means that you are writing words that promote someone else's and it won't fit your specific product line.

- If you do a mailing and it produces $XXX profitable results (this assumes you keep track of your customer names and as much detailed purchase history as possible), never wait 3 months to mail again. You can go right back to that same list the next day and pull 50% of that list. If follow-up with a phone call, you'll multiple response by 6 times or more. You can tell them that they are preferred customers (or haven't been in for a while or whatever), you wanted to reiterate the details and tell some kid of bonus, like since you're letting me discuss this briefly with you on the phone, I'll give you 15-day free trial.

Mailing Your Products

- Put extras in all order boxes that you send to customer to reduce returns. Customers love unexpected gift(s). For expansive items, perhaps send a small gift so it arrives the day before the ordered item to prepare the customer for the actual order and to make the customer anticipate the item even more. These tactics help reduce buyer's remorse.

Edited, Compiled, and Improved by Greg Perry

Money

- You need multiple income streams. Find several ways to sell your product line. Then find various ways to sell complimentary products. (The best income stream should be your control promotion and each subsequent promotion should be matched to see if another product or promotion out-performs the control. If it does, then that becomes your new control.)

Newsletters (Online & Physical)

- In your free or paid newsletter you send online, always provide an autoresponder sign-up link. If your letter is good, people will pass it around and you'll get new sign-ups this way.

- In a newsletter or marketing letter, longer is almost always better and almost always gets read more. (As long as you're informational and write in small sentences and keep the reader moving forward.)

- Remind people in their newsletters to update you with their new email addresses if they plan to change email addresses soon.

- If you want people to click to your web site from your newsletter, have great bullet points that lead into the web article so they have to click thru.

- Do not spam. Always give more value than your customers pay you.

- Always offer a P.S. with a restatement of your offer or some neat additional benefit.

- Don't just send a price list with cheap prices or a brochure. Tell the story of the customer who has and enjoys your product. Or of the customer who stopped a huge problem due to buying your product or service that avoids that problem your customers currently have.

- After *each* and *every* sentence, ask "Who Cares?" sarcastically as a hesitant customer might ask when reading it.

- All bullets should generate curiosity.

- In your routine educational letters, consider putting a link to a referral/affiliate product once in a while where you'll get a commission if your reader clicks and buys.

- Consider starting your *own* company's affiliate program. Check out two online giants in the affiliate business: Commission Junction and Rakuten Marketing.

- At the end of a newsletter each week or month, say "Hey, <first name>, expect another newsletter from me in 3 weeks."

Edited, Compiled, and Improved by Greg Perry

Newspapers

- Use *FSIs* (Full Sheet Inserts) which are those pieces of colored paper folded inside newspapers. Readers might skip over full page ads but they must physically handle FSIs. Plus, they're usually much cheaper than full-page ads.

Edited, Compiled, and Improved by Greg Perry

Objections

- If you get *I don't know* on any question that a potential buyer should know, respond with, "I understand but... what if you did know?" or "Sure, but think about what might be the case if you did know."

Edited, Compiled, and Improved by Greg Perry

Online Order Forms

- On order page, keep in mind that most typically lose orders right here. Do something to keep potential buyers interested and moving forward as they check out.

- In a newsletter with product offerings they can order, the final page at the end of the order should take them to a related site that has complimentary services and products you don't yet offer. Make sure it's an affiliate site (where you get paid for your referral if a purchase is made; your customer won't pay any extra for buying there).

Edited, Compiled, and Improved by Greg Perry

Order Forms (Online & In Person)

- Test this, but be sure to try making *all* order forms canary yellow. Often nothing else works as well. Canary yellow is like the yellow on legal pad pages. So when you hand out order forms at speaking events or training classes, use yellow and see if it bumps up your average.

- Even online order forms often look good and grab attention when yellow.

- Your order form should always be a small sales letter. Even if you just get an email or first and last names, every time you ask for *anything* utilize marketing skills to reduce customer hesitation and buyer remorse.

- Never bury an order link way down a web page that sells something. Put it several places throughout (not overdone) so buyers can quickly jump to it.

- Make the order button red. "Don't know why, but it has been tested to convert better," says one marketer. Marc Stockman advises adding a red, moving arrow that points to the order button to call attention to it.

Orders

- When selling on the Internet, *test this* because for some unique and expensive items, especially where the buyer may have last-second questions, it outpulls in many markets: Only allow people to order by phone! It really can outpull Internet-only orders and Internet/fax/phone/mail orders for large-ticket items.

Edited, Compiled, and Improved by Greg Perry

Payment

- After a customer orders online, always offer some kind of post-payment option, such as another free gift or an audio welcome that contains "3 most important ways to use your item..."

- To earn buyer's trust, you can ask for a post-dated check that you cannot cash until the buyer has had a full XXX days to check out the product. Or you can agree not to run the credit card through until after a certain date. This lets the buyer try the product without risk before spending actual money and can be perceived as being better than offering a guaranteed return of the product for a full refund.

Edited, Compiled, and Improved by Greg Perry

Photographers

- Consider trading referrals and coupons to wedding cake bakers, wedding planners, and so on. You'll often meet future wedding couples at the weddings you photograph.

- You need to become a supplier of throwaway cameras for wedding customers, as well as any gathering who hires you. Have a box for the cameras to be dropped into. Charge for the pictures for those who drop the disposable cameras in your box. Yes, even today with ubiquitous cell phone cameras, people appreciate actual, traditional developed photographs but hate the idea of going to a film development location to get them made. Also, the disposable camera could be digital and these developed photos are still often in demand. People at personal, large events will still often want actual photographs that you can develop from the digital prints. You won't get rich from this, these disposable cameras will add only a marginal profit to your business. But it's another income stream. And a relatively small marginal increase in profit over a year or more adds up to significant income that wouldn't otherwise be there.

Postcards

- 4 by 6" is best size. Anything larger is okay too (but more costly) because it stands out in the regular mail.

- Post cards are perhaps the *only* mailing piece where you can get away with labels. Hand addressing them appears to be a *complete waste of money*. People seem to accept a label or direct address printing on postcards more than they do on letters. Printing addresses directly on cards is a good idea to try too and you don't have the cost of the labels.

Edited, Compiled, and Improved by Greg Perry

Press Releases

- If you send a photo with a press release, send it as 4x6 color. An action shot might be better or a head shot might be, depending on the story. When getting your picture taken, pay extra if you have to so that *you* can have the negatives or JPEGs (up to $50 isn't too much). Always put name, address, phone, and PR headline on back of the photo you send. For action photos, describe all action (tell, don't sell).

- The preferred Press Release format (special thanks to Paul Hartunian) follows.

Deviate from this format at your own risk:

FOR IMMEDIATE RELEASE
CONTACT: (Real
(or a time qualifier)
person's name & phone #)

Killer (centered) headline that arouses curiosity and forces the reporter to keep reading

Section 1 - These few sentences should tell the reader what the *entire* release and story are about.

Section 2 - Quotation and credentials – Provide one or two quotes from yourself or other appropriate person and add that person's credentials.

Section 3 - the "call to action" and contact information.

(Center this at bottom to signal end of the P.R.)
# # #

- Tell and never ever sell in the press release. The quickest way to get your press release tossed out is to sell. A press release is to inform, inform, and then inform.

- Being outrageous is often a plus (being a nut is not). Often, your release is less outrageous than you think it is so feel free to work this up. Not all press releases should be outrageous but outrageous headlines and points are often great.

- After *each* and *every* sentence, ask "Who Cares?" just as you ask yourself this when writing any ad copy or headline.

- All press release bullets should generate curiosity!

- If you fax your release, never fax a bio or sample Q&A sheet. (The Q&A sheet are actual questions the interviewer might ask you; interviewers are used to getting Q&A sheets and really like it when you do their work for them.) (They can and almost always do ask other things, but your Q&A gives them a headstart they appreciate.) If you mail or email the release, always mail a bio and Q&A but be sure to put the release on top.

- Only send a *one*-page press release, 8-1/2" by 11" size only, white paper only, and no graphics other than a possible photograph you include.

- Never embed a photograph inside a single-sheet press release.

- Put "For Immediate Release" in upper left-hand corner or a time-qualifier like "For Release on or before September 8th" or "For Release between July 1 through July 31st"

- Upper-right hand corner's first line: "For further information contact:"

- Upper-right hand corner's second line: A real human being's name and direct phone number (either *your* number or your assistant or your voice mail that you say you'll get right back to the caller).

- You need a headline that sucks the reporter in and forces him to read your press release

- The second section of body copy should be a quote and that quote should *always* be from you! Never quote somebody else (unless it's an expert and known testimony that is powerful). Let them anybody else send out their own press release.

- If you are promoting a product using a press release, make sure you solve a problem. Every product solves a problem!

- Never lie in a press release.

- If you get publicity from a well-known celebrity or outlet, use *that* as a reference in subsequent releases or make it one of your bio items.

- The body copy has 3 sections:

  1. Tell *whole* story in 2 to 3 sentences.
  2. Quote yourself and include your credentials and qualifications.
  3. Your call to action (you want something to happen). As you write this section especially, after every single sentence, even one-word sentences, you should ask yourself (you know this by now, right?), "Who Cares?"

- Never single-space your entire body copy (you *might* single space here and there, such as indented short text.)

- If it's an informational general announcement such as a bake sale, find a theme for the event (keep thinking about the Editor who must fill blank columns of the paper or website ever edition).

- A perfect way to get on a radio show quickly: As soon as the host announces that there will be open phone lines in the next hour, *immediately* fax (yes, they will still have a fax) your press release with a brief note that says: "I just heard you say that next hour you're going to have open phones. In case that's the last thing you actually prefer, I've got a great topic you and I can discuss for the entire hour. I'm faxing a press release and Talking Point Questions along with this note to explain my topic. If you'd like to have me on, I'm ready *right now*. Call me at (XXX) XXX-XXXX.

Edited, Compiled, and Improved by Greg Perry

Pricing

- A Great line before a price: "And how much am I charging for this xyz item? Absolutely *nothing*...unless you are completely blown away by its results."

- When using dollar amounts, include the zeros ($x,xxx.00) if you're announcing how much money will be saved. Omit the commas and zeroes if you're talking about cost. The comma and .00 makes the number look bigger. Paying money is a pain trigger, so drop zeroes and commas (and don't even include the dollar sign when stating cost if it doesn't make the statement look too strange).

- Put the price in a slightly smaller font than the item's name next to the price (don't make it too obvious you've done this so as not to look manipulative (which it sort of is)).

- In your offer, give your buyers two or three price levels (*Good, Better, Best*) to attract a range of buyers. Buyers who want to pay the Good price will almost always move up to Better, when given this choice.

- 7's in prices normally do not do as well as they used to, but 9's do well. Test this of course. (Online products are often an exception.)

- $9.99 is far more of a draw than $10.

- Which works better, x.99, x.97, x.95, x.77? The number in the cents place seems to be insignificant, so use .99. But again, test this because your product or audience or selling venue might respond differently from the norm.

- Reduce the size of the .99 from the font size of the dollar amount.

- $99 is far better than $100 and $99 (or just 99 if the price location is obviously the price) is better than 99.99 or 99.xx

- Being cheapest is rarely the best long-term strategy unless you're huge and can take advantage of scaling. If you can't be the cheapest, it does you *no good* to be the second, third, or fifth cheapest. If price is to be a factor, therefore, be the *most expensive* and set yourself apart from the crowd by explaining early and often the advantages of going with "the best."

- When you position yourself as the best, people will not price-compare you. They will judge you on your quality.

By the way, if this is your goal, it's a respectable

one and a goal that can make you wealthy. But… you need to *be* the best at whatever you promote yourself as the best in. For example, a heater installation company might just sell routine, name-brand heaters. You can't honestly say your heaters are the best around. You *can* say that your service, your speed, your guarantee, your add-on products, your twice-annual free inspection, any or all of *those* are "the best." Focus greatly on those.

- Price too high? Create a volume discount and give them a year to do it. If they don't meet it, tell them one more quarter to make it up.

- How to evade "Your price is too high" is to have a generic clone. This is a product that's similar but downgraded from your primary product that you can sell for less. Perhaps give the buyers, if they upgrade, a full credit on the larger purchase so the clone is risk free. (Actually, all you sell should already be risk-free because if they don't like it, they can return it.)

- Have you thought of *blowing away your competitors in service and customer care* and not worrying about having the lowest price?

- In your sales letter, don't promote your product but instead, tell your customer what he gains or solves with your product.

- When you make your offer, always offer a bonus.

- Use *you* and *your* in everything you write.

- Longer letters typically work better... if they're not boring.

- Have a large ad that brings mixed-results? Place a smaller ad inside (a "star" ad) that sells something else. See what happens. Follow-up the sale with the back-end advertised in the big ad.

- People at the top can specify and describe their uniqueness. Others at the bottom of the market talk about price. If you can't quickly tell your clients why they should do business with you, you're at a disadvantage. You only have about 20 seconds (shorter for men, a little longer for women) to make your USP known clearly. If you can't do this, then you'd better have the lowest price because you're not going to compete otherwise.

Products

- Under-promise and over-deliver. If you think an order will take 7 days to arrive, promise buyers 10 and do it in 7. This gives you a day or two extra if something happens to delay the order.

- If you need a new product to sell this month, to keep things stirred up and to look in demand and busy, you can look to affiliate programs and endorse one of those products or services if you can't do one of your own. Look at fast-food signs; every month or two, they have a new whiz-bang item on their menu. This is almost always just a reconfiguration of ingredients from their regular menu but the new item draws people in who would otherwise not.

- Use eBay and Amazon to sell products once you're a distributor. Never ignore these outlets or you ignore a huge potential income that takes virtually no work to provide once your item is listed on the two sites.

- Here's a back-end idea - a live audio session with you teaching your client something. Better? Start your own podcast and work it.

- Don't worry about your back-end until you test if your front-end item will sell.

- The moment someone buys your front-end, send an email with a discount coupon and if they pass it along to someone to buy with that code, you will reimburse the first buyer $XX.

- Make sure you have a truly valuable coupon of some kind that they must tear out of a book or manual that's worth using when a customer buys a product from you. State it must be the original coupon torn from the cover page (best) or first page of the manual or paperwork inside. Customers are less likely to return the product if they've torn something out of the paperwork that goes with the product.

- Do the work for them - for informational products, people really don't want to learn how to do something but instead they want it done for them. Some or most of your products should be forms or step-by-step advice so they don't have to think.

- Shrink-wrap your products in cellophane. You'll have fewer returns because people feel more like they own something when they open it.

- Niche everything! Once you successfully market a product, start niching it to a specific group. Generate leads from that group's magazines or whatever and target the product towards them.

- Put your picture on *back* not the front of product. The photo personalizes the item or company but never use a prominent location to plant your picture. Buyers don't care about you and you add nothing of value to the product. A short bio or company history, with your photo or the photo of your employees interacting in a back location can personalize the business, however.

- *Always* have a spine (title on the spine) of *any* media product that goes on a shelf (book, audio, or video) so that buyers will know what your product is on their bookshelves.

- The spine should read with the letters rotated properly, unlike most book spines. In other words, the title's letters on the spine should not be rotated left or right when your book is in their shelf but should read top-to-bottom as it sits on the shelf. Although physical bookstores are far less important than they used to be, if your media item ever gets in bookstores, your item's title stands out from the rest that are rotated to be read only after the book is pulled from the shelf and flat.

- Every product *must* solve a problem (when being sold) to be effective.

- Do you have a high-value product? Have you considered sending, to your good customers, a $50 restaurant gift certificate along with an inexpensive USB drive or CD, and if they promise to listen to the entire recording about your newest offering or upgrade, then they can have a nice dinner on you with no obligation whatsoever.

- Do you upsell with a complementary product and as you do, you teach your customer why it's such an important add-on product?

- Yes, this is odd. That can make it powerful. If you sell a disposable product, such as a pool chemical, you could place a plastic-sealed $3-$5 cash at the bottom of the container with a note saying, "You can use this cash to purchase your refill!" Some buyers might use it faster to get the cash! If not, it's a powerful message to remind your buyer that you exist and that you can supply them with exactly what they're out of.

- Your product is too hard to understand? Never! You need to have a script that can succinctly explain to people on a short elevator ride what your product does for someone specifically.

- How many people sell your same product or service? Your answer should be *nobody does* and you should be able to tell why instantly and honestly and accurately. Find out why you're unique. Ask your customers why they buy from you, you'll be shocked because it's almost *never* why you think is the reason.

Promotions

- Use testimonials. When you get enough, get more testimonials.

- For more traffic: Put your web address on a plastic magnetic sign on your car, get one for both sides, also for your trunk. Put your cell number on the sign because everybody you drive by will a cell phone. The magnetic signs can be made locally (FedEx-Kinkos) or on websites. They are reasonably priced. Follow all ad copy rules when you design the sign, but you're more limited in space on the car sign than you normally will be. Make sure your phone number and web site domain name are easily visible. (To save space, put MyComp.com instead of http://www.MyComp.com)

- Offer freebies (lots of freebies and if possible, place maximum time-limits on the freebies' claim to increase the buyer's urgency). Always tell *why* you're making the good offers.

- People love free reports. But also free CDs, free videos, free newsletters, and so on.

- Your buyer's second-favorite word is *free*. (Your buyer's first-favorite word is *you* when you put it in ad copy and promotions.)

- Upsell the moment of any actual sale. Consider offering add-on products, a larger quantity discount, a special companion product, whatever you do, upsell *something* at the time of the actual sale. This is true, perhaps even more so, when your buyer checks out online.

- Make sure your sales staff has a line of upsell items that they can offer in typical circumstances when the client has decided to buy but before actually paying.

- A possible upsell is an in-depth consultation (or two consultations within a year's time) inside your store with no obligation. "Strictly an educational consultation." This gets your customer back in your store to buy again. Also, many won't even make the appointments so it will not be a time drain on you, but if every customer *did* return for the consultation, that's a great thing and shouldn't be viewed as a time drain but a promotion that got a previous buyer into your store that you didn't spend a cent to get back. You could also sell an annualized service contract and include the current price of the current service being bought. This will be a profit even though some will call for your service the rest of the year more than others (i.e., carpet cleaning or pest control.)

- Free services for front-end and leads are okay, but they do invite lots of freebie-grabbers. It's better to offer a free service, such as a free inspection, to discuss needs of your potential clients. Also, free items are great to give away and don't seem to generate the same freebie-grabbers that services do. If you do have a valuable service that you can give away, consider contacting a charity and give proceeds to it. Charge customers for it, but 100% goes to charity. Make this a sideline service. The charity will promote your business!

- If you ignore $2,500 of upsell or cross-sale potential at the point of each sale in a year, then you have just removed a *real* $2,500 from your business's coffers.

- See if there is a National Speakers Association to sign up for you to give free or low-cost informative speeches that provide solutions. Offer a free report to anyone there who gives you a business card.

- Consider this expense-management strategy: Pour all your excess money into marketing and pay a supplier extra for delivery. Don't tie up money in inventory. It's better to pay a slightly-higher per-item price when you make a sale and need a product to deliver today or now.

- Want to make some money as a marketer? Write 100 businessmen who advertise on billboards, fliers, and use yellow pages in your area. Send them a letter via FedEx that you would like to write a sales letter, contact them in person for a 5-minute interview, find out if they have a good-selling product at a fairly good margin, offer to sell it for XX% more if you keep a percentage of the extra. You can get his customer list (don't consider pirating the list), send a letter FedEx to his customer list with a sales letter for the product (this assumes one costing several grand), have a private showing to those companies, be there and collect your commission.

- On your bonuses: (some states have laws governing how bonuses can work, check into it). Instead of saying they only get the bonus if they act within XX days or whatever, say, "I'll only guarantee this free, jam-packed bonus for XX days." This way, you haven't said they won't get the product at the end of the time frame, only that you guarantee they'll get if it they act that quickly.

- Want a celebrity for product credentials and validity? You can in the "Academy Players Directory" from: Academy Of Motion Pictures Arts And Sciences, 8949 Wilshire Boulevard` Beverly Hills, California 90211, Telephone (213) 278-8990. By the way, of the 1,000 actors and actresses who you know of by name and/or face, fewer than 200 can support themselves through acting alone. If you write your bid for the product endorsement and send it to the agent listed in that book, the agent is bound by ethics to present your offer to the client. A letter from such a star (with a huge picture on the letter's letterhead) will get noticed. You not only get the people but you get the added "reflected glory" by legally listing all the shows and movies and magazines (use all or some depending on your product) they've been in.

- A great bonus to include is a session of email-based consultation on any single subject/problem they are having. (Make sure they know you cannot answer legal questions, unless of course you're an attorney.) Most people never take advantage of an email-based consultation. "You have up to 2 years to do this!" This bonus alone is worth more (in consultation time) than the price of most front-end projects.

- Send a personal postcard (sign it) and say you have an important recorded message telling them the "5 Things they should know before buying a…" and have that recorded message on your machine or website play link. It should have *real* informative information. Also, a "private" phone number to reach you directly and/or your business address to show products or services you have if "they need the product or serviced immediately." Of course, sending them to a web site is better, especially if the web site is a sales letter with a signup box for a newsletter.

- You can also have people call a 900 number ($2+any toll, or whatever) to listen to an educational promotion (be sure you *really* give them valuable information).

- Determine and only then address the needs of your prospects. Do not decide what the market wants or will respond to, find out what the market wants and then respond.

P. S.

- As you surely must know already, all sales copy should have a postscript (P.S.) The P.S. gets read almost every time, even from those many who skim the rest of your ad or sales letter.

- Your P.S. should restate guarantee, premium offer, or the major benefit.

- On the P.S. use a hanging indent so all lines of the P.S. message are positioned to the right of the *P.* and *S.*

- Podcast-related P.S. – Yes, even if you record podcasts, you can provide a P.S. for your listeners! Sean D'Souza perfected this technique. On many of his podcasts, his closing music (the "outro") will begin and play for about half its usual time. He then interrupts the music and ask, "Are you still listening?" What this does is make those who *are* still listening think they're part of an exclusive club. No doubt, at least half the listeners would have stopped by then. Those (of us) who stay the whole time get an added bonus, one we really listen to just as a reader of sales copy reads the P.S. of his. Over time, Sean D'Souza trains us to expect it so the more you listen, the more likely you are to join that exclusive club and the more listeners he will have who look forward to that interruption.

Public Speaking

- When you make a presentation (i.e., informative sales pitch), speak a little too fast and give too much information. Doing this increases your back-of-room sales.

- On the back-of-room sales: Your sales staff should greet people *enthusiastically*; a smile is not enough.

- Make sure your price list of goods on the back table is passed out right as you begin discussing the items you have for sale. Tell them to take a pen or pencil (do this with them) and cross off the prices as you say, "The retail for all these separately would be $xyz, my combined discount is $xyz, but cross that off and write a special for this seminar which is $xyz!"

- Speaking: Always speak right before a break! After going over product list, say "Mark either A or B (or C if you offer three options) and take your form to the product table before your break. We have several product packages here, but we can ship them to you if you don't want to take them with you today. If you want your items today, be sure to go straight back there to get them after we're done here. If we run out though, we'll ship to you within 72 hours, but I know how people like to take either some or all their product with them the moment they pay. - After the break, I'll be around here and you can ask me questions and I'll be glad to autograph the book you get if you want." All of this is pre-suppositional that they will buy products. It gets them in the mode of already owning some of the things you're offering at the back of the room.

- About your back-of-room products: Make them look like specialized products. For example, use a pink insert if you're selling to a Mary Key convention.

- Sell multi-sets, never individual discs. When a customer is offered too many products, he buys nothing.

- Back of room products - Have 2 or 3 things to choose from *only*. These are complete packages. For example, on my non-fiction writing packages, I'll have a low-end and clearly state that it's for people who have never written, who don't know how to write, and who don't even know if it's for them. Then, my intermediate package is for people who already have the desire to see their published book, the best ways to make that happen, and massive tools that will streamline all the processes for you except the actual putting of words together in your mind. The advanced course which is for those who want to maximize their writing income and truly approach this as a business as a way to make a very good living off their work, who not only want to see their books published by the major houses but also do the profitable self-publishing route.

Inside *each* product needs to be a do-it-for-you kind of solution. They don't want to be taught, they want the work done for them! When anyone wants individual items, tell them that you cannot do that as a professional because you don't want them to fail. You didn't put together the packages except to give them every tool they need to succeed. Create a rush to that back table! "I could only bring a limited number... Come up with a *really* hot bonus that is *only* with the big package and say you only have ## [about 20% of the audience, estimate number] and so only the first few are going to be able to do that one. You need a rush to the back table - perhaps only the first ### get to phone in on your teleseminar in three days where you reveal something so new you haven't had time to develop a product for it yet, and that's probably good because the price of your products will have to increase so dramatically when you get this one done but you'll give a the first XX a call-in slot for free on the teleseminar where you announce this very thing.

- Pay anybody who works the back table an upsell incentive percentage of all upsells they make. Teach them to be sincere, like glance at order form when they turn around to fulfill an order and say, "Oh you're just getting the intro... did you realize that the full package costs only $NN more and you get $XXX in bonuses *plus* $XYZ worth of consultation?"

Publicity

- When doing radio interviews, try to get WKXW or really *any* Trenton, NJ station because it's the most people coverage of any place in the nation.

- Free classified is available on Internet. Search for "Free Classified" to locate them. Often they'll say they give you free ad for seven days but it's often left up long after that. If you find free advertising on specialty sites that focus only on one topic and require ads related to that, then tailor your ad to *that* market. These may not be as plentiful as they once were but they do exist and are *free*.

Edited, Compiled, and Improved by Greg Perry

Receipts

- Every receipt you give can have a small questionnaire for testing. Instead, or in addition to a questionnaire, you can also ask for their email address for free specials.

- Bounce-back offers are critical like coupons on your receipts.

- The entire back of most store receipts is blank. *Why?* If yours are too, you are throwing away a free advertising space for a coupon bounce-back offer that almost every buyer would otherwise see.

Edited, Compiled, and Improved by Greg Perry

Referrals

- Tell your current customers that if they refer somebody else and come into your business with them, both your current customer *and* the referred potential buyer will each get 50% off any item or service you sell. (It's fine to limit this to a certain dollar amount, but don't be stingy.) This works well in hair salons, car mechanics, and other places.)

- Create a host/beneficiary relationship with another, complementary business. Perhaps they send their customers mailings, so give them coupons to put in their mailing for your business. Give them a percentage of all use of those coupons. Keep this in mind for your own vendors as well so that perhaps you can include such a coupon/referral and get a percentage of those sales you refer in your mailings.

- Don't rely on random referrals even though this may be a huge reason for new clients. Have a formalized referral system in place.

- If you don't know your customer's marginal net worth, you'll always skimp on a referral system because you'll under-estimate the value of a referral.

- Train your entire staff in your referral system. Have scripts available to learn.

- Follow up on *all* referrals you receive. Then follow-up again. Then again.

- Think through where *your* customers go for the goods and services and this is how you get referrals and trade coupons. For example, a photographer should trade referrals to wedding cake bakeries.

- If you're in a strip center or shopping mall, offer to provide gift certificates for the other stores to send to their customers for your business. Give the business payment/commission on all certificates redeemed and offer to do the same.

- Have multiple referral-generating systems. Get customers to bring you more, get vendors to bring you more, and so on. They become your own extended sales team.

- Remember your vendors! Send business their way by rewarding your best clients with certificates for your vendors (no strings attached, free service, and so on). You don't need a payment; instead, just ask those vendors if they'll give you a certain discount off your next purchase for every sale they make through your client referral. You can tell your clients that you could send a holiday turkey or something but you'd rather give them a free, no-obligation service or product (from one of your vendors) that's really worth something special and real, such as a free two-hour consultation from your CPA who has saved you a ton of deductions, etc., and you want to pass this along to your better clients.

- Contact other non-competing businesses close by that sell to your same customer type and create cross-coupons you can both give out for each other.

- Not all referrals can be done the same way. Doctors, dentists, and plumbers can all get referrals from clients. But what if you're the middle man? What if you're a reseller? Retailers who buy from you are not going to refer you to their competitors so they're competitors buy from you, right? But that's okay. Why not give them a bonus for referring you to other retailers *not* inside their circle of competition or even inside the same region or state you're in? What about giving them a big bonus for referring you to non-competitors?

- Car dealers should have a free coupon from a locksmith who will make them two free keys for their new car, with no questions asked. That should be in the packet that you, the car dealer, gives the new client. (Think how this same strategy can work for any business.) Instead of the locksmith, you can mail a letter to the customer five days after the sale and handwrite on the envelop, "Here's your free spare keys" plus other coupon discounts, plus a thank-you letter, plus a short "How can I improve?" questionnaire, plus a referral card where you'll give a portion of referred sales to their favorite charity in their name or directly to them, and a note about how you will give them an better-than-normal trade-in if they re-purchase from you in the future.

Note: Sure, many newer cars use fob beepers and some are keyless. Still, a spare key or two is useful if they can't get in their trunk or car the normal way. The key won't start most newer cars but it will get them into the car if the normal, modern, more automated methods fail.

- When you refer or create a Host/Beneficiary relationship, you can be the conduit and transact their purchase through you. You can pay if the dollars are huge to place an operator on the other company's site, you can request an audit, all these details are available for discussion ahead of time. You can make the rules, you are subscribing to the Indiana Jones School of Marketing, you are the one who is generating the business, you control the situation, you're bring them the extra bonus sales. You can do two tests of the same kinds of vendors or beneficiaries and see if they pay you about evenly and if not, perhaps the low-paying one is shorting you. You always have good reason to audit.

- Perhaps you don't feel comfortable taking a referral fee? Get another that you don't take payment from along with one you do. Develop a relationship with the paying one so that you can help resolved disputes, so that you can step in if needed and make the client happy. Tell your client you have two people who can do the job, both are comparable in price and quality, but the one you have a relationship with and you can be an ombudsman for them and help resolve problems and you'll ensure and have power to follow-up if they mess up and make the client happy. The other you don't have that relationship with but they have promised to do the same quality of job. Remember, all things being equal, if you can help provide more risk protection, you deserve to be paid for that service.

Edited, Compiled, and Improved by Greg Perry

Rent Houses

- Accept credit cards for rent payments (PayPal is fine too, many younger renters have PayPal accounts, and for these who don't, you can charge credit cards through PayPal.) Do the following: Give tenants a form that states if the rent isn't received by the 5th, then you can automatically charge their credit card so they don't get charged a late fee or be evicted.

- Two credit card numbers are always better than one in case one doesn't go through.

- When buying new rental properties, find out how long a house has been on the market. Obviously, distressed is better. But savvy sellers know to take their house off the market for a short time and then relist it so they can say "it's only been on the market a short while." If you hear this, follow up with, "Have you ever tried to sell this in the past?" which makes someone feel uncomfortable if they've relisted it but asking won't bother those who haven't. If they answer yes, ask, "How long ago and why did you decide to relist it now?"

- When buying a rent house, figure it will cost 10% to carry including loss of interest on money you put down, property taxes, wear-and-tear, repairs, extras, and so on. Always factor in that your cost will *always* come to 10%. If you think 10% is too low for a specific property, you're paying too much for it.

- It's not self-promotion if it's true. If you find yourself in a Landlord or Landlady position and hate it, why not completely change everything using a tiny handful of steps to make being a Property Manager *simple* and *profitable?*

  Then immediately get a copy of *Loving Landlording: How to Get the Best Tenants and Make the Most Money Letting Others Buy Real Estate for You*, Amazon #B00I2CQ12Y, by Greg Perry (a wildly successful Landlord and Property Manager for 28 years).

Restaurants

- Send a weekly special once in a while to customers in your Guestbook-originated address list

- Hire young females, encourage her to have her friends drop in for discounted "Employee Acquaintance" snacks. Lots of girls ensure lots of boys. This works very well in a café or coffee shop situation.

- Send a menu once in a while to your customers and outline your current special, and write a note to the individual such as, "John, you need to try this" and circle the item. Tell John, "I'll give you a large sample free to try to see if you like it the next time you come in. I'm anxious for your feedback!"

Edited, Compiled, and Improved by Greg Perry

Resume

- Circle with a red pen one or more points in your resume that targets specifically the company you send it to. The person who looks them over will quite likely think someone else in the company had looked at yours and circled the items.

  Yes, many resumes and job applications are done online. But many are still performed the traditional way also.

- Put a paper clip on the right side of your first page. This seems to get attention and slightly increases the chance that the initial reviewer looks at your resume instead of just skimming it as quickly as he or she skims all the rest to filter out.

Edited, Compiled, and Improved by Greg Perry

Risk Reversal

- Of course, always offer a money-back guarantee, but explain it in detail, tell the customer exactly what you'll do if the customer doesn't like your services.

- "Risk Free for XX Days" is better than "Money Back Guarantee."

- The longer you extend the offer for a complete money-back guarantee, the *less likely* they will take advantage of you unfairly. This is an odd correlation but true.

- Better than "Satisfaction Guaranteed" is a "No-questions asked, 100 percent money-back guarantee anytime within 60 days if my product fails to perform exactly as promised with no hard feelings on our part." (And if you can even get more specific on the guaranteed performance details, it's better.)

- Make your risk-reversal so specific that readers will think you will be ripped-off by other customers that will surely take advantage of your product. This goes a tremendous way into telling your would-be clients they have zero risk.

Sales Closing Techniques

- The "Ben Franklin" (and Other Secret Ways to Close a Sales Pitch) By John Forde for Early to Rise:

"Have you ever bought a car from a dealer? If so, you've probably been hit with every one of the sales techniques cited below and then some. Likewise, if you've ever bought anything over the phone after a cold call. Or if you've ever purchased a piece of real estate.

Whether used in print or in person, sale-closing secrets seem to be the same. Or similar. Here are a few of the "classics" that you might be able to apply to your own marketing efforts:

1. The Ben Franklin Close
This is really just a simple, traditional persuasion technique. The only thing Franklin did was make it famous by actively applying it. Here's how it works: Draw a line down the center of a page. On the left side of the line, list every possible "minus" response your potential

customer could think of. On the right side, list all the possible "plus" responses. The longer the list on the right side, the more likely the sale. Use that list to reinforce your sales pitch and train your sales staff.

"Let me be clear on what I can't do for you.
"But let me also make sure you understand what I can offer."

2. The Buying-Criteria Close
Draw a line down the middle of another piece of paper. This time, the trick is to make a list of buyer needs and then counter each of those needs with the product benefit that satisfies it.

"You've waited a long time to lose those extra pounds. Too long? Not at all. Lard-Be-Gone works no matter what your age."
"You want to take better care of your heart. Lard-Be-Gone is fortified with 6 essential antioxidants, shown in a Finnish study to reduce heart disease by as much as 63%."

3. A Double-Whammy-Question Close
Starting to close to a sale with a question is common practice. But some sales professionals stack the questions one after the other. The first question is just a statement of something your prospect is wondering. The second is a challenge to the prospect to act, dependent on the answer.

"Is there any kind of 'safety buffer' on this

investment idea? If there were, would you consider giving my service a try?"

This could then be followed up with another benefit:

"This is the only drug company that's finished FDA trials on the drug I told you about. We're only 3 months away from full approval. And all prospects look good."

4. The "This-Could-Be-You" Close
Lots of promo pieces open with stories about people in the same predicament as the prospect. Sometimes with happy endings. Sometimes not. You can do the same to close a sale. For instance:

"Still undecided? Maybe hearing what happened with Mary Pritchett will help you make up your mind. Mary was diagnosed with diabetes 6 years ago. She started on a full course of insulin, special diet, and full exercise schedule.

"14 months later, she started to lose her eyesight. Her limbs fell off. Her hair turned purple. Mary thought she was too far gone to be helped.

"Desperate, she tried Kidney-Kickstarter and was as right as rain in less than 4 days.

"You're probably in much better shape than Mary right now. But why take chances on what the future holds?"

(You get the picture.)

5. The "Feel, Felt, Found" Close
Sales folk widely credit Zig Ziglar with this one
- a simple statement to help overcome lingering
objections. For example:

"If you're thinking this isn't the first time
you've heard promises about vitamins and
arthritis, I know how you feel. I felt the same
way when I was having joint troubles of my
own.

"But then I found bio-chemically activated *Flex-O-Rific*, and everything changed almost
overnight."

Just be warned before you try any of the above
that closing a sale is a little like shooting pool:
You shouldn't try to put a spin on the ball until
you've mastered the straight shot.

- Re-visit the basics: justifying the price,
  removing risk with a guarantee, always giving
  one more reason to buy, and so on. Find a way
  to get excited about the product you're selling.
  And look for ways to get your customer
  nodding his or her head throughout the pitch.
  Let him feel that the decision to buy is his
  decision, rather than something you've imposed
  on him.

- Don't go after the big sale all the time. When going after big clients, don't say you're a financial planner and you're selling financial planning, say you're giving a free seminar on financial planning.

- *Do what you need to do to get the first sale.* The less time you spend on your first sale, the less time it takes to get the back end.

- For excess inventory you cannot get rid of, tell your customers *why* you're selling (won't have more for a long time or ever, we have a full inventory for the final time, bonus if they act now, otherwise more later, only offer to best customers first (and really do this), or to first time customers get first choice, and so on).

Edited, Compiled, and Improved by Greg Perry

Sales Letters

- Your sale's letter's audience doesn't just want something to make their life easier, they want something that will make them happier, richer, thinner, and better than most other people. Tell your clients how your product or service will give them the status they crave.

- Your ad/letter should *always*: Lead with your offer's major benefit! Don't ever stray from this fundamental rule of all sales copy. Don't bury your most important benefit thinking it will surprise readers. Without it at the top, most of your readers will have stopped long before then.

- The word "that" is often a copy killer. Take out all of them if the sentence can still make sense.

- To know if a sentence requires "that" or "which," the word "that" can *always* be removed and the sentence will still make sense. "Which" is sometimes required to keep a sentence accurate and you won't be able to eliminate the occurrences of "which."

- Have an 8- or 9-year old read your sales letter. If they stumble on any part, it's got a problem and you need to edit some more.

- Overcome all objections. "Here is why many people tend not to buy/trust these kinds of products..." then take care of the objections.

- A professional head shot photo in a sales letter can increase sales, perhaps because it generates trust and shows you're a real person. But use common sense and don't do it if you look like a thug. And never, ever use a photo if you have a beard. Some of the population refuses to trust anyone with a beard.

- Can have a fold-over "Read this only if you're still saying No" and say, "I find that in talking to 1,000s of customers that there are only 3 reasons to say "No" (take care of all three) (although you already did so in your sales letter, this is all just a restating... or perhaps, written from your wife or secretary).

- A good control is 10% of your population. Send control to 90% and send changed letter to 10% to see how the 10% pulls. That's enough for testing a control.

- Each page should have an arrow with a note saying, "Turn to learn my secret in..."

- If price is a problem, address it head on.

- Every offer, ad, letter needs a summary recap pitch. "Now remember..." or "Let's summarize..." or "for $___, you get ___ (an irresistible offer)"

- Must have punchy, active letters. Never be boring.

- In the urgency, give them a reward or penalty for hurrying. Don't fib, give a valid reason ("We only have 1,000 to sell") and make it clear that it's available now but not forever. Use "Takeaway selling" by explaining that not everybody's going to get to get in on this.

- Your order form: First person: "Yes, Greg, I'll take advantage of this..." "Rush my..." (never say "send"), "My name is:" "My address is:," etc.

- Sample guarantees: "If your neighbors don't start asking you how you're making all this money...I'll refund $$$."

- Put questions throughout the letter that *always* will generate a *yes* response. You want to get them used to saying yes for the close.

- Start the close from the first word in the letter.

- Try to deliver the same benefit argument throughout the sales letter, slightly reworded to work. You want to plant that benefit in their minds and you catch those who skim and start reading halfway down.

- About the only place you don't use the standard AIDA sales letter formula is on billboards. All other places, including business to business (B2B) use the same techniques.

- Put lots of sub-headings throughout your sales letters. Each sub-head should stand on its own.

- Photocaptions should work just like headlines. Don't just say, "Here is Jim and Joan in our office." The picture's job is to get the reader to read the headline and the headline is to get them to read the ad.

- Always read your sales letter out loud. If you ever say "So what?" or "Why cares?" after any paragraph, toss out the paragraph or edit it greatly.

- Always read your sales letter out loud. If you stumble over *any*thing, then you've found where your greased funnel is missing grease. Edit, edit, and edit.

- An intriguing story is perhaps the most important element possible.

- Think of someone you know who would fall in your targeted sales letter audience. Someone in your life or that you've known. Write to that person! You will have an automatic rapport that you would not otherwise have!

- Sales letters or web sites should have testimonials but make sure they are typical of what the average customer will experience. You might even put a reasonable disclaimer there.

- Don't ever end a page in a multi-page letter with a period, always do mid-sentence page endings.

- Always add a footer in the lower-right that says, "Go to next page" or "Go to page 2."

- It's best to end each page with a cliff-hanger ("Not only will I reveal how to double your income in 5 days or less, I will also...")

- Have your letter's first P.S. upsell something that costs 25% of the deal. The second P.S. should reiterate the time-limit offer.

- Numbered lists are *super* in marketing letters, signs, ads, "newsletter mailings," such as "12 Reasons Why You Need..." or "8 Things You Should Do Before You..."

- Your letter does not have to end with a plea for money. Perhaps just click for a new report or a bonus. For large sales, this can help qualify your customers faster for you; doing this definitely educates them better when needed.

- All your letters should sound as though they know your clients. As though you've been listening to their phone conversations about problems to solves and wants they have. Understand your clients and let yours words show that without it sounding like you're selling.

- Use the letter's P.S. to upsell with another product add-on (25% of the price), or to reiterate your guarantee

- Grab them with your opening in the letter to get them to read more. Grab them all the way through. Sell your product, don't allow any cloudiness. You are selling them. People won't know the value of your product if you don't sell them.

- Don't sell too many products. You may now be selling 20 items in a mailing. Sell only one or two at most.

- Keep sending your letter or postcard until it stops working. Go ahead and send to the same people if you want.

- Make analogies constantly, like the "Joe Montana of cashbacks" or the "Wayne Gretzy of accuracy."

- You can also metaphor movies "The Jedi Knight of Landlords!"

- You can start a metaphor by, "A friend of mine had a problem that was XXX and here's how he solved it. Knowing this, you also can solve it by..."

- You can start your letters with so many kinds of grabbers - Take this test!, Damaged Goods Must Go Cheap, We Want to Give You a Free Trial, Here's a Limited edition, A "Tale of Two People" letter, etc.

- It's worth repeating: Always offer a P.S. with a restatement of your offer or some neat additional benefit.

- Don't ask if the client needs or wants your products and services ("Have you been thinking of investing in stocks?") but assume that your prospects are desirous of your goods and services. The typical sales letter *asks*, you should *state*.

- Online ordering: Easy forms, explain what secure means, sprinkle Submit buttons all over so they don't have to scroll to bottom, provide fax, email, mailing address, and phone order numbers.

- Your action request should be a right-away kind of request.

- Provide an all risk-free major benefit in your letter.

- You need more bullets. Then, add more. Every detail of your product needs one somewhere in your letter.

- Sample bullets: "3 Questions you MUST ask before…" "How to get EXTRA …" "The single best way to… and to do it FAST" "A dirty little secret that XXX hope you never find out!" "Why adding XXX can DECREASE the value" "Seven questions you should ask IMMEDIATELY before…" "How to gain a razor-sharp EDGE in negotiating.." "Six Things to do if your XXX is not selling FAST."

- Make *every* word count in your ad.

- Have lots of *How To* titles in your chapter titles that you sell as a course. "How to Get XXX (specific benefit)…," "How to Avoid XXX (specific problem)…," "How to Get XXX (specific result)…," "How to Get Rid Of XXX (specific pain)…"

- Extended bullet often is good, "Embarrassing litter-box odors (You may grow used to them but your guests *will* notice them) "

- Reverse polarity bullets are effective: "Eliminates embarrassing little box odors (You feel comfortable and at ease when guests come over because you *know* there are no offensive or sickening odors)." The words before the parentheses are positive, the parentheses are negative or vice-versa.

- Use "you" and "your" a lot in ads and direct mail.

- Always use a headline in direct mail to customers. Always have an offer. Always have a risk-free trial. Always have a limiting time-frame.

- Find out a problem your customers have that your product or service will solve. Make your headline address that problem.

- Have an action line at the bottom of your letter. Tell your customer exactly what he can do and tell him how to do it.

- State a large value of your product if you were to sell the items in a package separately. Be realistic, informational products can have high perceived value but you must be realistic. Your own time in a half-hour consultation is worth a ton.

- In your sales letter, say something like, "Don't buy XXX Product unless it meets These 5

Tested Criteria" and then make sure your product is the only one that really fits these criteria.

- Have *lots* of How To titles in your sales letter bullets and in your eBook chapter titles that you sell as a course. See Headlines.

- Many bullet points should appear before your price. Increase the perceived value of your product before hitting them with the cost. Compare the price to what you used to sell for, what you will sell it for or what your competition sells for.

- Always present your new sales letter that you send to your customers (perhaps a sales letter that you include with a routine information letter) that shows the customer you've done work for them and will save them money (or time or headaches or something else). Never make it appear as though you're stuffing new products down their throats.

- Sales letter free bonus items can be in dark blue headlines to help develop trust

- The "How To…" headline is often good. Make a specific promise in your headline. Make the first sentence grab the reader to read more. Talk about your customer, not your product. The headline is to get them to read the first line. The first line is to get them to read the first paragraph. The first paragraph is to get them to read the entire letter.

- When you use lots of bulleted items, also use red checkmarks for the actual bullets to see how it pulls over regular black bullets.

- For your company web site, the purpose should be specific, such as generate a phone call or an order. Your web site should generally not be your primary marketing tool (obviously some Web-based businesses are exceptions).

- Been in the field long? State in your report and letters your years of experience unlike your competitors.

- "Preemptive positioning" is the practice of immediately explaining why you're giving such a good deal, perhaps spending a fourth or half of your sales letter telling the reader why this sounds so good. Tell the reader (this also applies to *all* negotiations you do, even verbally) what's in it for *you* and then give all the reasons why this benefit the reader even more.

- Never *lead* a sales letter or ad with testimonials. It makes the item about *you* and *your product* instead of about the *buyer*. Scatter testimonials throughout, and then scatter even more, but don't lead with testimonials. It's far too early.

- Your headline should make a specific promise of an end result. Your headline should often use one of these words: You, New, or How. The first paragraph or sentence should be only one or two sentences long. First sentence should talk about the reader and *not* about your company or your products. Explain the benefits the reader *only* gets from you if he makes this decision. Explain the benefit of every product's feature. Talk specifics, not something like "dependable or reliable." Present compelling proof that you can deliver. Summarize benefits with numerous bullets. Actually, compose the majority of your sales letters with bullets. Reduce the sting from any price with bargain appeal. Give free bonuses or a price discount for acting before a deadline. Ask the prospect *not* to make a decision (risk reversal), just to try it and you'll take on all the risk if there's any reason why it doesn't fulfill your promises.

- Ways to hold interest longer in long copy:

1. Start some paragraphs with such questions. They help change pace and style.
2. Give copy news value, fresh news to the reader is always welcome.
3. Avoid vague generalities; be concrete and tell who, what, when, where, and why.
4. Stick to buying points, concerning the reader, not selling points concerning the advertiser. Sell people advantages and not things.
5. Always include lots of emotional appeal.
6. Touch people so they say, "Yes, that's just like me!"
7. Avoid flat claims but paint vivid portrayals of dramatic situations.
8. Use subheads having news or curiosity appear.
9. Use short, simple sentences.
10. Use vivid present tense, singular instead of plural. Make it already happen to him as

your readers read. Let your readers see themselves doing it.

11. Use active verbs and pictorial nouns.
12. Avoid too many adjectives, adverbs, pronouns, demonstrative articles, dependent clauses, and phrases.

- Subheads act like ladder rungs that a reader can drop down to. Use plenty of sub-headings to break up your letters.

Sales Staff

- In addition to finding your top one or two or three sales people and making them train others to do the same thing, also break your sales staff into other various segments such as those who generate the most by phone, the most cold calls, the most in person, the most out of town, the most in a certain area or region, and for each of those items the best in each group should teach all the others.

- Reconsider giving your sales staff too much autonomy. That's probably a mistake. This isn't a democracy it's a business. You want to know what the good people do and what the bad salespeople do and you want to cull the bad things and multiply the good things that work.

- When someone calls, how prepared is the *first customer contact person* to handle the call? What about browsing shoppers in your store who ask employees questions, do you have scripts prepared?

- Do all your sales staff sell the same amount or do two out of ten sell the most? If so, shouldn't you find out what those two do and train the others? Don't you want *all* of them to sell just as much?

Seminars and Webinars

- Change "enrollment forms" for seminars to "applications" that they must "qualify" to be "accepted." Making it more difficult to enroll often increases enrollments.

- When "live" such as at a seminar, create a one-on-one bond within ten seconds and then build on it! If they smile, you then smile. If they say hello, you then say hello. If they offer their hand, shake it. You have affirmed their actions and have affirmed they can trust you. And you look over to your left over his right ear any time you wish to speak directly to his sub-conscious. You have identified yourself as a "friendly" by this person and within minutes they will share every aspect of their life with you.

- The "Unconscious Hello": Put yourself in a neutral state. Don't go up to someone smiling, laughing, sticking out your hand. You contaminate the evidence! Go neutral. Instead, say hello without emotion (light friendly) and *pay attention* to what they are doing with their face, eyes, heads, eyebrows, head, and whatever they do, do it back to them after a tiny pause. There will be a flash of recognition and they will typically smile. When you get that second acknowledgement from them, look over their right ear. Don't do this extremely quickly or slowly, just mimic naturally. (You look over their right ear to *anchor* it. When you are ready to ask for the order, what do you do? You look over by their right ear and they get the feeling of trust reinforced once again and then you ask for the order.) But, this "trick" won't work unless you practice and do it always.

- The mimicking seems simple – it is, do it. They will not think you're mimicking them.

- If they answer a yes question but shake their head no, they don't want what they said yes to. (And you should respond the same way, such as shaking no but saying, "certainly.") You also learn how they are doing their "yes's" and "no's" and you can track that throughout the rest of your conversation. *Ignore all sales advice to shake your head yes as you ask and interview the other person.* You'll contaminate their responses and you'll falsely read their responses.

- Constantly calibrate their yes's and no's.

- If you get no responses (however you learned how they telegraph them), you don't move to the next section of your sales or close. Back up and approach again until you get a yes. Wait on them and keep them all along when you know they are with you – only then can you move forward.

Service Businesses (Plumbers, Electricians, Hair Salons, Pest Control, etc.)

- On your web site or email every once in a while, or your yellow pages ad, have a letter available (in printed form also) that says, "Warning! Don't Use Any Plumber Until You Read This!" then explain why you are the only one they should do business with.

- Most clients wait far too long to get their next service. You need to be in charge of setting up your clients' next appointments and sending reminders and calling them about that next automatic appointment. It's a service that you need to ethically train your clients so their car/hair/health/whatever runs smoother between visits.

- If you sell a service such as training, do you guarantee that if your customer doesn't make their money back in XXX months, you will refund everything? (as long as they tried by XXX)?

- Your services can be a gift. This is an incredible way to get front-end business. For example, if you are an attorney (or CPA or chiropractor or whatever), a friend or businessman who is *not* one can give to his clients a gift which will be *your* services, free for two hours for example. He can send an introductory letter to his clients introducing you, saying "I normally send a basket or something, but this year I want to give more to my best clients this year. Mr. XXX has been a top-notch XXX for me and my partners/family/whatever and he has my full trust. As a gift to you this year, I have bought $XXX worth of his services and he has offered to double those services (or whatever) for you. You can use this gift and never use him again, nobody will expect follow-up business. This is truly a gift to you that I think actually has far more value than the $XXX that it's worth."

- Offer a x% discount for lump-sum payments but offer extended payment schedules also, like "4 easy payments of $XXX."

- A good guarantee for service clients: if you don't like what we've done, we'll redo it. If you still don't like what we've done, you pay us nothing.

- Tell your customer that he pays only if you do what you say you'll do. Especially for service work.

- A routine service, such as a hair salon or pest control, can offer a free initial service (or two or three) if the customer buys a pack of coupons for their next dozen services (less the first 2 free makes that only buying 10) at a discount over what the 10 would cost normally. Or an oil change. Offer to telephone or postcard the clients when the service is due. (Upsell once they come in.) Your marketing costs for these subsequent sales is *zero*.

Edited, Compiled, and Improved by Greg Perry

Signage

- Ask your customers, and the better they are the more reliable you can determine, about your signage, both large and small close to the walk-in door. Is it all visible? Does it generate a reaction you like? Anything missing?

- It's often helpful to ask *new* customers about your signs also. Maybe even better, they will see things that old-timers miss. Offer a free item if they spend four minutes walking outside helping you evaluate your signage.

- For roadside banners outside your business, use white background with black letters. Some experts say dark blue letters on white background. Use what you think is the best of either but nothing else.

- Magnetic signs are very good for your cars for advertising. And if you travel to another town, just take your sign with you and stick it on your rental car. (This assumes you have a national business or a Web site. Or want one or both.)

- If you have a company with signs on the buildings, you're foolish if your phone number is not on the outside sign and building. Every car that drives by has at least one cell phone in it.

Surveys

- Do surveys often.

- If you ever need survey info from your opt-in list, send a survey and a free offer if they return the survey.

- Send surveys to sample customers in your target audience to find out what product or service they want (not necessarily need) and do this before you flesh out or develop your product line. Give survey of 12 products and see which they want most - this is your lead product!

- Send employees regular questionnaires but make sure they always remain anonymous so you get more accurate answers.

- Use surveys to find out what customers want, make it simple, a simple email, offer bonus for customers filling it out. Survey the price, attitudes, products, and wants.

Edited, Compiled, and Improved by Greg Perry

Target Customers

- Don't think you can locate where a group you want to target lives? There are magazines they love, rent its mailing list!

Edited, Compiled, and Improved by Greg Perry

Telephoning and Telemarketing

- If someone calls cold and places an order, consider having a script close to the phone for any staff member who answers the call. Once the sale is complete and the details are over, before hanging up, if it's another business who's the customer, consider asking them that in case they do business with you in the future, perhaps they would like to be part of a special business list you keep confidential, for special intra-business sales. Also, offer to be on their list if they have a similar one.

- Telemarketing only works well when you prepare the way with a mailing. And cold telemarketing to unknowns is best left to the experts.

- Don't have a bank of sales takers in a telemarketing call—in order-taking system. Have a sales system. Train your staff to be a part of the business, give them a piece of the pie, show them the importance of cross-selling and add-selling.

- Do not cold call! It's inefficient. Follow a mailing perhaps, even better after some other lead generator, but don't waste your time.

- Cold calling is the most difficult telephone "strategy" that exists. It's inefficient. Follow a mailing perhaps, even better after some other lead generator, but don't waste your time cold calling unless you are one of the few who have rare expertise in how to perform this feat successfully.

Testimonials

- Constantly collect testimonials.

- If you don't ask a customer for a testimonial, you will not get a testimonial.

- At the end of a survey, you can ask if you can use the info in the survey if you can use the notes, and the name, or perhaps initials only (if they gave name).

- Use as many testimonials as possible. Even in an informercial or advertorial, 18 minutes of testimonials in a 25-minute video isn't too many. This is known as the "ponderance of proof."

- Consider this for your initial testimonial request template: "I've never written a letter like this before and I may not write a letter like it again. But I just met a man/service/product (or I used something or something just happened to me) that I was so is so profound and I was so impressed with that I had to tell you about it. Go into explanation of person/his product, what is so unique about it, etc., it's so important because your people are probably as exasperated as we were and you worked this out for a blank-benefit, it's normally but they right now get it and this bonus. I stand behind this completely.

- Printed or displayed testimonials are more effective with a full name, city, and state.

- Use the term "Verified Testimonials" (whatever that means).

- If you're just starting out but have no product testimonials yet, use personal testimonials such as "John is the most _____ guy I've..." Also, look for quotes (quote web sites are full of them) about your product/site's emphasis such as "Taking action..." or "Making money..."

- When online, frame testimonials in red on a yellow background.

- Change to "What others are saying:" which often sounds better than using the trite "Testimonials" title.

- For online sites, use the tab Kind Words instead of Testimonials or What Others Are Saying. It should generate more hits due to curiosity.

- Picking testimonials – Dan Kennedy says that testimonials identified only by initials are worthless. You need people giving testimony to be real and believable with names, occupations, ages, cities, states, details, details, details.

- You can't always get approval for full name, age, city, state, and so on. Whatever you can get your testimonial writer to approve use it. The more demographic information you can include, the more powerful it will be. But even if a first initial is all you can get, use that.

- If you own a physical business, create a Wall of Fame Thank You Noteboard for customers who've written thank-you notes to you. Customers like to see their writing there. Also, it's a powerful, better-than-advertising method for all you do because it's a wall of testimonials that fellow customers are saying about you.

- Testimonials should be very specific such as "I went to car dealer A and it cost me $10,200 and I went to car dealer B and it cost me $9,200 and then I went to Car Dealer C and got a deal for $8,500 – I saved $x,xxx." Superlatives like "great" don't work. It's fine to close with, "I don't see how they stay in business at these prices!"

- Always ask for a "before and after" testimonial. Better, give the customer a small, 5-question survey. At the top, explain that they will get a free item if they take a moment to answer the questions. The first question should ask what they originally wanted from your business. Walk them through a before-and-after scenario. When done, you will often have a "this is where I was and these are the changes and benefits I now enjoy because I bought this item or service" and such is a most powerful testimonial.

- Seek and publish testimonials, ask customers for their opinion and get their approval to publish their opinions.

Testing

- Never assume you know what your clients want. Survey and test consistently and constantly.

- You have absolutely no right to determine what the market wants - but you have a duty to find out.

- Don't let your testing take away from sales and other tasks. Tests don't have to be extremely time consuming and scientific all the time. You'll spend too much time testing and not enough time responding to your tests.

- Statistically, 30 or more replies on anything (list, ad, promotion, mailing) then you have a good sample for testing. If you get 15 then it drops to 70% and below so you really need to get 30 or more responses (no matter how large your population is) to consider it a meaningful test.

- Test *every* idea you have time to test. Don't try a newsletter or email letter without a way to test the results. You can do this with a link that includes a number for each customer you send

to and the Web site will send that number to
you telling you the email just was read by that
customer. You can provide just enough info in
your email to excite the customer to click for
the details.

- Your test can be small, even 100 or so. The
critical thing is that you receive at least 30
responses however. No matter how large or
small, you have to get 30 responses to be
statistically valid. (40 is marginally better, but
probably not worth extra effort if you get 30+.)

- "Key" your test responses. use a different
phone number in yellow page ad than from
drive-by number, use online coupon codes, add
"department 7h" for clients who call from an
ad, if you send letters to current clients for
repeat business use two telephone numbers for
two headlines to see which pulls the most.

- Your ad will cost $XXX whether it works or
not. So test headlines! Use two ads with two
headlines and try to determine why one worked
better than the other. Then re-word other items
to see what brings maximum results. Perhaps
one's guarantee is better or one's price works
better.

- Make sure ads bring in starter clients that
actually purchase. Some ads bring in fewer
clients but generate far more purchases and you
must test this. You must track:
(a) Which ad brings in sales,
(b) How many orders a given ad produces,
(c) How much the average order is worth,

(d) How much a client or order costs,

(e) How much or how many times the client reorders, and

(f) How much money a given ad generates or loses

- Test your product, your sales staff, you scripts, your store, and your suppliers. Send in a plant that is the toughest customer (a "secret shopper" who could conceivable exist and go through it and see what the results are.

- Test everything you try. Use different headlines in ads and letters, see which works best. Use different phone numbers (see Yellow Pages section), different email addresses, and so on.

- A different theme every night would work for a café or bar. A different offer each week or month would work for other kinds of business. By doing these things, you test what works best for your organization.

- Instead of sending out a large postcard mailing, first send out a set of three or more samples to test which works best for responses.

- So you send 100 people mailing and only get 25 responses. You send another 100 people mailings and only get 25 responses. It's better to send to both groups, 200 people, and get 50 responses to get a better test the next time.

Edited, Compiled, and Improved by Greg Perry

Trademarks

- Use little TM in your title (common law trademark), also get ® which is federally-registered trademark.

- The government's trademark site allows searches - often you can find a match but can still register!

Edited, Compiled, and Improved by Greg Perry

Tradeshows

- Tradeshows – Your booth's banners are your headlines and initial ads for the booth. Don't be the 75% of booths walked by (everyone who attends a trade show normally ignores 75% of the booths there). Forget your company name! Let people know who walk by exactly what you can do for *them*.

- You must have the ability to pre-market tradeshows. You need to have the list of attendees or at least last year's to farm for leads through direct mail or email if you can ride the tradeshow's emails. A great technique is to send one-half of an extremely nice pen with their name on the cap and tell them to stop by the booth to pick up the rest of the pen!

- For building a business or starting a new one: Go to a trade show in your targeted market of expertise. Locate the smallest booth with a great product but with an owner who doesn't know how to market. Get resell rights and sell the product.

- Right before a potential customer walks away from your booth, hand them a bright, shiny penny and tell them a bright, shiny penny saved is a bright, shiny penny earned. Then, when you follow-up within the next five days on the phone, you can remind them that you're the one who gave them the bright, shiny penny and you want to guarantee them that they will view their new product (your product, of course, a kitchen remodel or whatever) is just as bright and shiny as that penny. This costs about $10 max per show and increases a customer's contact memory dramatically.

Trials

- "Try Before You Buy" is more powerful than "Free Trial" and "Half Price" works better than "Half Off" or "50% Discount."

Edited, Compiled, and Improved by Greg Perry

USP (Unique Selling Proposition)

- If you want to know what your USP is, one of the best ways is to ask, "Why does my best customer buy from me over my competition?"

- Another effective USP-generating question would be, "Why do customers buy from my competitors and not me?"

- Have a USP (Unique Selling Principle) to distinguish your product. To learn your specific USP, here is a way to start: "Most businesses in my industry do XXXXX but I do YYYYY." You can ask current customers questions that enable you to find this. (Then, turn those answers into testimonials.)

- Your USP must set you apart. Your business should be built at every level around your USP.

- Wrap emotion into your USP.

- Consider this when determining a USP: "McDonalds (change business as needed to match one like yours) spends millions of dollars getting your customers - don't compete with them, improve on an aspect of the business they can't or don't do well."

- Your USP is not price. Perhaps it's the best quality or quantity at the best price, but sell results and not a low price. Only the giants can compete on price for the long-term.

- Your competition can be beneficial! Once you know your USP and you know what you cannot do that your competitor can (differences always exist), go to the competitor and ask if they can white-label some work for you if your customers want something that requires the competitor's difference. They must not attempt to take away your customers and you can reverse all this as well for them. Suggest joint ventures for the things you and they offer that are different.

- Once you know your USP you may be able to license it to others, or train others in how to do it with income to you.

- To develop and test USP you must have the answers to these 3 questions:

  1. Why should I choose to do business with you vs. any and every other option available to me?
  2. What do you offer that no one else can or will? (or What are you known for?)
  3. What is your reason for existence in your chosen market - other than the fact that you want to be there? (or What do you *want* to be known for?)

- Find something your competitors do very badly and target that. Like when Dominoes targeted bad delivery times.

- 3 Key USP elements:

  1. It has to have a direct or implied benefit. It must say "buy this product and you will get this particular benefit."
  2. It has to be an important benefit -- important enough to "move the masses" (or at least move your prospect).
  3. The benefit must be one that the competition either cannot or does not offer.

  If your USP has all three of these components, there's a strong chance your direct-mail package will be a success.

- Do all of your employees, *every one of them*, know your company's USP? If so, do they continually live by it at work?

- Many businesses craft a USP that describes *what* they do but not *why* a customer should do business with them. A what-only USP isn't a USP but is a business description. It's fine to use initially if you don't know the answer to *why* a customer should buy from you and not from somebody else. But you need to get your head around why people buy from you fast, and you need to exploit that why and train the public with it inside your USP. That takes a tagline from "business description" to USP. The what *and* the why.

Note: Some companies don't need the *what* included in their USP. People already know what pizza delivery services do. Many smaller businesses, especially small service companies, often need to put what they do as well as why customers should buy from them inside their USP. This is a bigger challenge to do but it makes the USP even more important for them.

- Using your USP, telegraph to your customer base and to the world the reason why it's to the customer's advantage to deal with you instead of the competition, the alternative, or doing nothing.

- If you do have a USP, is it clear to your customers? If not, make it clear to them in all you do.

- When determining your, try several until you discover the most important approach and your most powerful USP.

- Your USP may even be a picture, a headline, just some competitive advantage. FedEx's was "when it positively, absolutely, has to get there tomorrow" and Domino's was "30 minutes or it's free." Those kinds of statements can be powerful USPs. It's better to control and lead the market with your USP than to follow. And you'd better be able to deliver and personify and project your USP throughout your organization. Your people and all your company resources *must* be congruent with your USP. Your USP must be flowing throughout your organization to show that it's not just lip service.

Edited, Compiled, and Improved by Greg Perry

Vendors

- Share with your referral vendors all client information. Never violate any client agreement in doing this, however. If you ask for email and promise never to share or sell their email addresses, then stick to your promise.

- Remember your vendors. Send business their way by rewarding your best clients with certificates for your vendors (no strings attached, free service, and so on). You don't need a profit, just ask your vendors if they'll give you a certain discount off your next purchase for every sale they make through your client referral. You can tell your clients that you could send a holiday turkey or something but you'd rather give them a free, no-obligation service or product (from one of your vendors) that's really worth something special and real, such as a free two-hour consultation from your CPA who has saved you a ton of deductions, etc., and you want to pass this along to your better clients.

- Good for retail businesses: Make a packet that includes true discounts from the entire circle of vendors, all vendors share weekly the list of clients so a master list can be kept by all vendors. This is an extremely timely way to get the info between vendors. Let the circle of vendors know if an address correction is needed.

Web-Based Sales Letter

- At bottom of your 1-page web page, have another opt-in link to your newsletter. Make sure you have the entrance pop-up as well. Autoresponders, such as Aweber.com do this for you. You can use cookies to pop up only a few times if your site is one that clients frequently visit.

- 65 letters max per line of email and Web newsletters. This limitation is less critical than it used to be, but many email users still opt for text-only emails and by limiting your emails' line lengths to 65, you lower the risk of badly-formatted emails arriving in some of your clients' Inboxes.

- Sell online? 24 hours after the sale, send an email asking if things went well and even offer a free bonus. Give them customer service information. Tell them something about their product that you didn't mention before, such as a unique use for it. Also, offer another sale. Four days later, do it again.

- Use a one-product, one-page site, at least for front end product. You want to have affiliate programs and it's much easier if you sell only one product on one site and also you don't want your affiliates selling your back-end products.

- Your web site should probably just have a killer sales letter selling one product. Your routine letters to clients will refer to this site.

- If you want people to click to your web site from your newsletter, have great bullet points that lead into the web article so they have to click thru.

- Any "free report" can be nothing more than a list of resources that your target customer can use (web sites, finance options, etc.)

Web General

- Build traffic via eZines. Write articles on related blogs for free publicity. Get articles related to your expertise in all major blogs that allow for guest writings.

- If you have a web site, and you're a small business such as plumber, you want your web site to tell your potential clients about what they want to know, more than you can possibly give them when they're in your store or when you're in their home. Have specials regularly, tell them in detail *why* they should do business with you but do it in why it's their benefit. Have training and tutorials galore, lots of info on how they can avoid you, put elimination tips in your sales letters such as ordinary and safe things your client can fix themselves that they'd normally charge you. One electrician's special may be something like, if a customer has a broken lamp and they bring *you* the lamp, you won't charge a service call and you fix it at a reduced rate.

- On any web site, you want them to buy, leave email address, or leave.

- For any Web site more than five pages or so, a search engine is a must and it must have allowances for misspellings.

- Always load up the first few lines of a Web site's home page and window's edge text to be filled with keywords. This helps get seen in search engines.

- Keep your home page and window bar's text not only filled with keywords but keep in mind that in a search engine's results page, potential buyers will be seeing them too. You want to use them in strong copy to get them to click and read more. Make them talk so anybody who sees the words in Google will want to click there, don't just list keywords in the title bar, for example.

- On your web site or email every once in a while, or your yellow pages ad, have a letter available (in printed form also) that says, "Warning! Don't Use Any Plumber until you read this!" then explain why you are the only one they should do business with (Great for used car salespeople and other perceived risk businesses)

- *Never* say "Welcome" on your home page!

- Your Web can have a "Bargain Table" for overstocks and discontinued items.

- Good blog or eZine article (keep all of them rather short): Tell a personal story that reveals a problem you were having, tell how you discovered the solution, lost the benefits of the solution, Give the solution as 4 to 8 simple steps.

Edited, Compiled, and Improved by Greg Perry

Yellow Pages

- Yellow page ads *are* still relevant for local businesses. Your ad should have multiple reasons/avenues for action. Perhaps one phone number for information sent, a 2nd for recorded, non-threatening information, first-time customers can learn more about you here, have client testimonials here and refer to the other number for scheduling. Also, push them on this phone call to leave their name and number if they want you to call them and the best time to call, or for a free report (describe the report), also you want an email address in the Ad and your Web site where you collect as much client info as possible.

- I believe in big ads in the Yellow Pages. I also believe in small ads, called in-column ads, in the Yellow Pages. These ads should be used to direct readers to your big ad. The best placement for an in-column ad is early in the category listing. These ads are arranged alphabetically. Ah, ha! If your business begins with the letter A… or you can create an alias too for the yellow pages!... The name of many local businesses begin with A to appear first in the Yellow Pages.

- These tips work best for those businesses whose yellow page ads produce the most success in that industry, i.e. plumbers get most first-time business from yellow pages.

- Provide a letter (in printed form and email also) that says, "Warning! Don't Use Any Plumber until you read this free report!" then explain why you are the only one they should do business with (Great for used car salespeople and other perceived risk businesses)

- The ad should be plenty large enough to provide a free offer - Such as a free report (via email autoresponder) like, "11 things you need to know before you call [whomever]" Actually, offer the report to anyone who calls, but put an email link in the ad such as, "To receive this report within 15 seconds, send an email to: [whatever].kbot.com" (Yes, you need to be able to send it in hardcopy form also to anyone who wants it.) You now have his name and address or email. If you use an autoresponder, use a sequential autoresponder to follow up the next day, "11 *more* things you need to know before you call [whomever]" - the next day, send a coupon for a special discount or free something, free consulting, no strings attached, "We won't try to sell you anything, we want to show you we care about you and want you to be happy and fully understand whatever situation you're in. *but* if you decide to use us for anything, we will give you XX% off the price. This discount applies to our normal, everyday low price, not to some phony inflated price that we'll tell. you get this discount because you called us to explore your problem and we want to thank you for that, but if you do not need or want any of our services, consider our consulting/whatever a free gift." Follow up regularly, with monthly specials or whatever. To test effectiveness, use a separate phone number for your email ad. (See below.)

- Advertise in more than one yellow page books (many exist in most locales). Put a different phone number in each. Put a third phone number in your white page alphabetical listing. Track calls to know which produces the most results for when you renew your ad the following year.

- In yellow pages, use a business-like type face like Times New Roman or Garamond. Do *not* use a Helvetica-like font as it looks commercial. You want to portray "trust trust trust" and *not* "buy buy buy."

- In the yellow pages keep your company name small in your yellow pages, business card, or *any* ad. A client doesn't want to contact a company, he wants to talk with someone who will solve his problem. Feature your personal name, perhaps high even right after headline. Even a small photo with your name, perhaps a quote like, "The buck stops at my desk" or something more specific to show readers that you are taking responsibility for their solutions and they aren't dealing with answering machines all the time.

- The larger ad sells dramatically better. Make yourself look like the biggest game in town.

- Never allow a customer call to go to voice mail. Get call forwarding. (Caller ID will let you know which number they actually dialed?)

- Google Voice is a superb phone service that is still free to use at the time of this writing. You get your own number in your area code that you can forward to one or more other phones. You can block numbers. You can change any of the forwarding numbers. If you change phones a lot because you move a lot (such as a journeyman might do in different seasons), you can change the Google Voice number to forward to your new number. Your callers never know they're actually calling a different number.

- Test different price points - your customers will NOT complain (generally) and the few that might, just explain to them that you need to find an appropriate price and immediately give them the difference. That's the great thing about a list - you can send one half a product for one price and the other at another price to see which works better.

- If you're having trouble selling what you sell, you may be selling the wrong thing to the wrong folks. Survey your list (give something for their answers), offer 12 potential products and see which they like best. You can rent more targeted lists if you want to try a more targeted audience for your wares but don't test/waste using the whole list.

- If you need a back-end, you can bundle products from several vendors into one, for a fair price, and you have a unique product because you'll be selling the package.

- Make your yellow page ad look like an editorial with a great headline.

- Start your company name with A to be listed first.